Think

Like a

Molecule

Seeking Inspiration In

The Structures of Thought

Chuck Champlin

CHAMPLIN MEDIA

ISBN: 978-1-64314-466-5 (Paperback)
       978-1-64314-467-2 (E-book)

AuthorsPress
California, USA
www.authorspress.com

To: Yvonne

May you be
inspired!

😊

Chuck Champlin
Wed. 2/25/23

Contents

A molecule might be defined as the smallest particle of a substance that retains all the properties of the substance and is composed of one or more atoms. It comes from the French molécule, from New Latin molecula, which is the diminutive of mass in Latin. The first known use of the word molecule was in 1794, according to an online dictionary.

Suggested synonyms for molecule include: atom, crumb, dribble, fleck, flyspeck, grain, granule, bit, morsel, mote, nubbin, nugget, particle, patch, scrap, scruple, snip, snippet, speck, tittle – also, assembly, constituent, agent, workhorse.

Can there be a "molecule of thought?"

*

When I was seven years old, my mother the chemist showed me a simple demonstration in our kitchen. In a saucepan of water, she dissolved a cup of sugar. Then, to prove that the sugar was still in the pan, "hidden among the water molecules," she placed the pan on a burner and boiled the water away.

Soon, what remained was a white powdery mess on the bottom of the pan. The sugar did not look like fine crystals anymore. But the point was made, and my imagining mind was lured down into the world of molecules.

My late brother-in-law and golfing buddy Charley often laughed at me when he could tell I was seeing the invisible connections between people and ideas, and he'd react with the mocking words: "Molecules, man, molecules!"

It is still true; I am looking for the synergetic connections, the influences seen and unseen, and the a-ha moments that make life so interesting.

Can you imagine the beginning of the universe?

Scientists and cosmologists – smart people who think about the cosmos – tell us that it all started with a "Big Bang," a super rapid expansion emanating from a single point that was smaller than the tip of a needle.

Fantastic as that sounds, that's what our best rational minds have come up with, which aligns fairly well with the Bible, where God said, "Let there be light." On the other hand, some cultures say the universe was sneezed out by a turtle!

I am afraid this book will not get us any closer to understanding our origin story. Maybe this universe is in fact a test-tube experiment by some Overlord curious to know what might happen with such an assembly of moving parts as the one we have. Our human imaginations will certainly play a role in determining the outcomes.

What I hope to do with this book is to encourage your imaginative insights about everything from science to God.

Many people on our planet "talk to God" every day, asking for aid or forgiveness, and feeling sure that such a mind could help.

While for me, the jury on God is still out, I do feel very sure that someday we will discover other intelligence in the universe. Maybe our prayers will be answered in such a convincing way that we will all believe it. Or perhaps the revelation will come in the form of space travelers carrying insights, or from our homegrown analysts who will examine every clue from a distance.

Right now, I can only wonder.

What I do know, however, is that this giant universal experiment, however it started, has after some 14 billion years, achieved a remarkable feat. During its enormous lifetime, the universe has created Life itself, and then helped us to evolve and prosper, with ever sharper and more expressive thinking.

As we think, the universe is thinking about itself.

To "think like a molecule" means to be aware of the physical foundations in matter that have given rise to our thoughts, and to apply some wonder to how it all happened.

Even more than that, the very structure of matter, from quarks and atoms evolving into molecules and everything that's around us and part of us, can inspire us to shape new ideas, new possibilities for our lives and our human civilization

Knowing that the universe has created us, and "taught us" to think, we are ready to speed onward, with hope, into realms of pure imagination and the twinkling stars of our potential for survival and prosperity.

1

THINK LIKE A
MOLECULE?

Can a molecule think?

There has not been much debate as to whether molecules can think. Despite their energy and complex structures, molecules most likely do not take time to ponder the ways they fit into the big scheme of things. They just *are*.

However, when many zillions of molecules bond into organized, functional systems, then we get everything – you and me, and some seven billion other thinkers and feelers like us in the world.

What is interesting about such molecular assemblies is not just the fact that physical matter somehow came together – possibly all on its own – to create life and thinking minds. It is also profound that our minds, born from all that accidental creativity, can now intentionally assemble marvelous new things using the materials all around us.

These seemingly trivial observations are worth some reflection. First of all, as when looking up at a starry night, it is inspiring to consider that so many functioning systems have indeed happened all by themselves. Moreover, we thinking latecomers to the Universe are starting to figure the systems out. Particle physics, organic chemistry and the operations of DNA and the human body are all about assemblies of atoms, molecules, and living cells, which the Universe has now evolved a way to think about.

Even today, after just a fraction of the life of the universe, new layers of systems are growing, thanks to non-accidental, mind-invented processes such as writing and reading, law, government, and the scientific method. These newest operating systems are now intentional constructions, born and operating in the human mind.

Most likely, such mind-made creations have never existed in the universe before. However, for most of us, conceiving in our minds that a human hair is about one million atoms wide is quite a surprise. It is another mind-bending fact that light, shooting towards us from the nearest star, spends four years traveling to Earth.

Casting our minds into realms of the very small – or out over vast distances to the stars – is a useful exercise. The effort can clearly bear intellectual fruit for all of us, by prompting mind-stretching analogies and new insights, suggesting new shapes and possibilities in our living world.

Of course, this is being done here on Earth every single day. The realms of biological engineering and media-based reality (e.g. Facebook), plus inventions like the ever-smarter smart phone, create real environments that support interconnectivities. These are new in kind and vast in their implications for (possibly) crowd-based future designs and creations – and for living together in efficiency and peace.

The fact that the structure of matter, starting at the atomic level, is fairly well understood by physicists and chemists has fostered fantastic improvements in the quality of our lives, our architecture, our powers of computing, and so much more.

But I'm arguing that, for the rest of us outside the realms of scientific eggheads, seeking insight, analogy and metaphor in the physical world can be inspirational in our lives, and in our thoughts. A-ha!

———

In the first chapter of this book, we visit the world of molecular science, ranging from the sources of such matter (star explosions and supernovas, where atoms were constructed); to an appreciation of the water molecule; through some basics about chemistry, and up through a view of molecular biology including DNA.

Somewhere in that spectrum, our physical universe crosses over from "inert" matter such as minerals and gases, to the realm of living things and into the physical realm of thinking minds.

DNA molecules somehow are a repository of human and animal knowledge, such as how to recognize a face, how to swim up rivers to spawn, how and when to protect territory, and how to recognize and capture food. Thus, it may be that DNA harbors or codes for some sort of a "will to live." That will to live, the will to prosperity, is even more alive and pronounced in our minds.

The good things that we want to bring into our prosperous world – such as more food for the hungry, homes for the homeless, new medicines and improved social systems – will be assemblies of elements and materials that we will build on the existing structures of our societies. The more we can implement systems that work well, to the benefit of all, the better off we will be.

Ted Sargent in his fascinating book "The Dance of the Molecules: How Nanotechnology Is Changing the World" (2006) notes that exotic new materials are increasingly being developed by scientists who consider what qualities are desired for the new materials, then analyze how molecules can be combined to create them. This talent grows directly from our evolving skills in molecular engineering and nanotechnology.

As Sargent asks: "Might the set of [molecular] combinations possible, and therefore the properties available, be far vaster and varied than what we and nature have fashioned thus far?" (Page 5)

Stronger, safer, more durable materials, and new technologies that employ them, are very much desired. But I think about Sargent's "vast and varied" molecular combinations even more broadly, to include people and their ideas. Examining the world of molecules can be a way to engage in some fresh thinking about our living, thinking world, social systems, and our collective imagination.

We already have vast and dynamic assemblies of thinking people, rich with ideas. They form the life of our towns, cities and nations. They build our corporations and clubs, and grow our communities. Many of the social groupings happen naturally, even by accident from chance encounters, or today through meet-ups on social media. However, the most effective associations are very intentional creations, for example, companies such as Apple and Google and Facebook, and cooperative systems such as sports leagues, media enterprises and movie studios.

As with the creative work on molecules by nanotechnologists, purposeful thinking about our individual roles and our social assemblies may help us advance the general welfare. That is the aim of this book. Thinking like a molecule means noticing how physical things and people come together, how they work in combinations, and imagining new ways that those combinations can be replicated and improved. Thinking like a molecule may give us new perspectives on things we take for granted and inspire new thoughts about the assembly of our world.

To support those goals, I am introducing a new conceptual tool – the Twinkle – a marker or asterisk in our thinking to help us develop our powers of invention. Thinking like a molecule invites you to visit afresh the world of your imagination, the thinking place where you observe and model the world.

For each of us, thinking is where our knowledge of the world really begins. We construct models in our minds that represent the places we walk and drive, the library of people we know, the stores where we shop. Then our language helps us identify such places and communicate with the people we meet there. Without such modeling of the world in our imaginations, and the communication to enable cooperation in dealing with that world, we would have little hope of survival and would have little more than animal instinct to guide us (though it's clear that even animals have an inner process of visualization and some skills in communication).

By the way, my definition of "imaginary" includes all the thoughts, images and knowledge we have in our minds. "You're imagining things!" goes the complaint. Yes I am; that's the way it is with my head. It's all imaginary.

While we try to make sure that the image in our "mind's eye" agrees with what's out there in the world, we cannot always confirm directly whether our mental models are in tune with those outside places. Sometimes a "real place" such as a molecule or the planet Pluto, must be largely imaginary or ephemeral (since we don't have the benefit of a physical reference). Recently, however, a space probe sent from Earth transmitted new photos from Pluto, and now the place is less imaginary, less ephemeral. Pictures showing ice-mountains and wide plains help to clarify

Pluto's geography in our minds. This is quite remarkable because we are not there at Pluto, not by 900 million miles. Likewise, tools such as the electron microscope, which uses electrons as the light source, are bringing us ever sharper pictures from the sub-microscopic world.

But, sometimes our imaginary visions are radically out of sync with the "real." In my dark and quiet room, I might say, "I feel as though it is nighttime," when it is broad daylight outside. My brain may be trying to represent "the way it is," but sometimes it can be very wrong! Good mental health is when the mind imagines "the way it is" in relatively close accord with the facts, which is what we are doing with Pluto – building a more accurate picture.

In a presidential race, the candidates and citizens argue about the way it actually is in our world today, and the way it *should* be. The dialogue draws folks into creating mental images of the way things *could* be, and of what we or our leaders should do to make things the way we want them to be. In the process, our thoughts exist on a spectrum of purely imaginary to visions that are accurate and up to date.

So, "thinking like a molecule" partly means focusing on and expanding the way we use our skills of mind to visualize things that are imaginary yet very real to us, such as "the health of the economy" or "the mood of the country." It also asks us to consider how that type of thinking might be improved, and even increase the likelihood that a clear and positive vision can be made real. It can be positive for all of us to get better at these skills of imagination, visualization and *reali*zation, because then more of us will be active participants in understanding, talking about, and taking action to improve the way it is.

The realizing part – making the vision real – is not always easy. When I imagine or intend that I will go to the store or meet a friend, the intention may be sincere, but the action and hoped-for result are not real yet. When I actually make the attempt, something happens. Maybe it's what I imagined, but maybe not quite. I may trip and fall on the way, or simply change my mind. The imaginary may become real, or it may work out differently from what I intended – just as Pluto turned out to have a different surface than the possibilities we considered.

The important idea for our future is that to some degree of certainty, our thoughts can be actualized. At the simplest level, we say, "I have an idea"; then we act, and some version of what we imagined comes alive in the world, or, the most elaborate systems are imagined, like Fed Ex, or YouTube. We are agents of future change.

How do we predict the chances of a certain outcome actually happening? If we think it through, based on logic and careful analysis – if we "look before we leap" – we may be able to get close. In principle, there is always some uncertainty – and that is part of the world of molecules as well. This is the essence of our eternal and universal questions, "What should I do? And, what will really happen if I do it?"

My goal is to help us ask and answer these questions, and thus to get better at creating a positive future.

Thinking like a molecule is an opportunity to notice the way bits and pieces of our world combine to make new arrangements, which can have important effects. Two hydrogen atoms join naturally with one oxygen atom to make a molecule of water. The way those three atoms work with each other, and the way the three-atom water molecule interacts with uncountable numbers of others, creates the beautiful and seemingly magical substance that served as the birthplace of life on this world.

A man-made "assembly" – my car – turns on with a simple key which sets the system in motion. It could kill someone if I'm not careful. Sometimes my pen creates influence with words, or buys something using my checkbook. These countless physical pieces of our world settle into patterns of utility. Then sometimes, they fall into disarray – the bathtub overflows, the airplane crashes.

Just as "imaginary" atoms and molecules assemble into our world, so do our tools and housewares, books and electrical systems, and our minds as well. Can we be aware of the many forms of cause and effect, the countless ways that we set systems in motion, sometimes for better, sometimes for worse?

By being more aware of the ways our imagination labels and manipulates reality, we can get better at these skills, and can induce success through stronger intuition and better visualization, better logic, and better planning, leading to more fully realized positive outcomes.

So, Meet the Twinkle

As I mentioned: in this book I am introducing a new tool for the imagination – The Twinkle – which I define as a conceptual marker for thought, like an asterisk or like the lightbulb that signals "There's an idea!"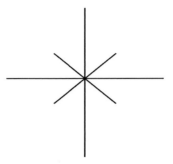

I use this tool to strengthen my awareness of a newly-arriving thought or feeling, the way a referee throws a flag on the football field to signify that an incident or foul has occurred during the chaos of a play. It helps him, as well as the stadium full of people, return to that moment afterwards and analyze just what was going on there. You can use the Twinkle as a tag when a concept, not yet fully verbalized or visualized, has appeared in the mind and may deserve to be investigated further.

A Twinkle can also stand as a framework for an as-yet-unidentified solution to a problem, something to "solve for" like "x" in an algebraic equation. You may create and name a Twinkle in your imagination to represent, for instance, "my perfect job" or "the way I will get out of jail." It's an advertisement for a solution, or an open framework on which an answer may be constructed (as we will discuss in Part 2, focused on The Twinkle).

Can you be aware enough of your own thinking (an act of "metacognition") that when a new thought arrives in your cranial space it can be assigned a Twinkle, like a Post-it note or a flag?

Noticing and marking a thought is the first step in developing the thought into an expression, a drawing, or perhaps a set of bullet points as an entry into writing. In my own mental imagery, the starry Twinkle shape may appear as a ghostly or semi-transparent image; but creating that simple additional thought-marker already helps me to illuminate and clarify my thinking.

Again, I will say much more in Chapter 2 about the uses of the Twinkle, but for now I note that the lighthearted name is intentionally designed to speak to the child in us, hopefully capturing something of the excitement and "magic" of a new thought appearing in the mind.

I consider the Twinkle a unit of "thought architecture," the start of a "geometry of meaning" flexible enough to define and represent new awareness, even helping ideas evolve into real things the way an architect's drawing can lead to a rebuilt world. Then, the Twinkle can continue to imbue that idea with the infinite potential it may hold, a library of the idea's growing dimensions. It's a tool frequently used by writers in developing their ideas, whether they recognize it or not. Notes and other bits of thought are labeled, categorized and organized into an effective whole that can shape the minds of others.

A Way to Be Aware

My intention is that the "Twinkle" will provide us all with a new reference point in the realm of the imaginary, helping us to bring forward inspiration into life here and now. My fascination with this tool springs from the fact that my life – and, I assume, everyone else's too) has been a continuous process of dawning awareness. As I age and mature, I grow to understand things that I never quite grasped before.

At age ten, I recall preparing for an airplane flight with my parents and siblings – the second flight of my life. I remember thinking: "Now that I am older than I was for my first flight (at age eight), I will be able to appreciate the experience much better." And I did take more notice of the bustling of the flight attendants, the safety announcements, the take-off, and the ground falling away.

This awareness of maturing and arriving at increased understanding and insight has always been a pleasure and satisfaction to me. I hope everyone has such learning experiences, and appreciates them as I do.

When I have this h-ha feeling, it's as if new buds of awareness have appeared on the branches of my pre-existing complex of understanding. A new structure of intellectual Tinker Toys is rising on the previous levels of comprehension, or like new branches growing in a coral reef.

I also recall that Sherlock Holmes, in one of his cases, commented to Dr. Watson that a good memory involves being aware of one's mental boxes and drawers in which ideas and memories are stored. Having a clear sense of our mental geography, Holmes was observing, means more confident access and thus improved memory. Also, seeing ideas somewhat as we see physical objects in the real world, makes them more real, more tangible.

We know that a car comes together as a functioning entity when all the carefully designed and fabricated parts are united in the working arrangement. Our minds are well able to visualize that system at work, so that when the completed vehicle rolls off the assembly line, when there's gas in the tank and the battery's charged, the simple turn of a key in the ignition or the press of a button will get the system running. We can see much more with the powers of visualization that we possess.

Learning does lead to system being understood, and then improved, perhaps with new features and user comforts. It also means that any conceptual structures such as governments, companies, families with needs, individuals with ideas or with dysfunctions – all these can be seen and understood more clearly, and dealt with more naturally as the dynamically functioning systems they are. Org charts are just one form of such a visualization process. So, humorously, are Rube Goldberg diagrams, complicated cause-and-effect scenarios that lead to a simple conclusion, such as a dog reaching to bite a steak, where the motion powers a backscratcher for the dog's owner.

To me, seeing the Twinkle as a symbol of dawning awareness (just before naming the thought occurs) is simply a new way to note and record a very common experience. Giving those a-ha moments a more sophisticated symbol elevates them to an enhanced status, a step closer to the physical.

My whole life has been about appreciation of – and some frustration with – systems that do or don't work well together, but which always grow and evolve. Luckily, I have had many moments of growth and insight. Now I want to preserve my experiences and learnings, hopefully with benefit for others. So ... I look at my experiences and try to comprehend them (as we all do); and, I write them down – a rich Twinkle process.

Allow me to . . .

To introduce myself to you, I will describe some moments and phases in my life, thinking of them as a string of Twinkles that highlight and label my life events and the evolution of my interests.

Phases of my life usually began with a time of questioning: "What should I do?" "Should I take this job?" and so on – a pro-and-con thinking flow that eventually created a new phase in my life. Each phase was undertaken with good intentions, often as a result of necessity or expectation; and, each brought me to new levels of personal discovery and hopefully maturity.

In addition to using the Twinkle process, the following vignettes illustrate how life frequently involves "molecular" processes that "bond" us to people and institutions, and ask us to respond to forces of change that push and pull us and cause us to act on our surroundings in combination with other people – similar to the way molecules form and break apart in evolving systems.

So, here is my life path, summarized (somewhat embarrassingly) as a simple a string of "Twinkles," here expanded with names and descriptions, that represent stages in my history, ticks on a timeline that can each be expanded with more information:

A Life, In Twinkles

* I was born October 28, 1950, and in seconds learned to breathe air – just one of the countless innate capabilities of the human body.

* I discovered and experimented with my body – with breathing, holding breath, crying, shouting, singing, communicating physically; learned about sleep, body rhythms, excretion, and other forms of my body's energy.

* I learned language under the guidance of parents, school and community. Another innate capability of my body, it needed to be activated and cultivated. To do that, the culture and people around went to work. I learned to read and to assemble words into writing.

* I learned to manipulate physical things. As a young person, I glued many plastic models of airplanes, dinosaurs and sailing ships. I learned to read plans and instructions, and learned thereby that I could physically shape the world. I learned that my internal mental images can be made real in the world through writing, drawing and construction.

* I grew in understanding that my father was a writer for Life and Time magazines (then went to the LA Times), but it was clear that he really *enjoyed* his work, and hoped I would find meaningful work, too.

* Explored home-construction sites in my neighborhood, gathering castoff raw materials for my own projects. Joined with neighbor kids like Chris Block, who led us in building a full-sized working set of an airplane in which we acted out adventure stories.

* Made a "fort" or shelter in the back yard – a paternal instinct? – posting my treasured photo of the young actress, Haley Mills.

* At 11, I undertook prayer that a pretty girl might move into the empty house next door, a sexual, reproductive and religious urge!

* Saw Disney's animated film "Cinderella," in which the Fairy Godmother appeared amid twinkling stars; learned the movie's songs from a yellow vinyl Disney record.

* Moved with family to London (1962) as my father took a job as a reporter at Time magazine. Fell in love with bicycles, along with my school friend, Simon Tilley (sadly now gone). Admired Simon's careful style of craftsmanship in our assembly of kites.

* Discovered music and the Beatles, the Who, the Rolling Stones, and realized that I wanted to be a drummer.

* Relocated with family back to Los Angeles for high school; I began to play and sing in bands, and learned I was good at geometry and math. Met my wife, Lesley (whom I did not marry until 40 years later).

* Finished an English degree at UC Berkeley, working for a time as a janitor. (My need to clean things and fix awkward situations I attribute to an occasionally volatile father.)

* As a drummer, I joined a good bar band in Los Angeles; I learned about the music business through a band manager, recording sessions, songwriting, and camaraderie with fellow musicians and families.

* Wanting to move beyond music, I moved into journalism at the Los Angeles Times (partly thanks to my father's job there), where I served as a "copy kid," sharpening pencils, then learning newswriting and editing, newspaper layout and writing articles about Hollywood special effects and technology, plus celebrity interviews and profiles.

* Left journalism to design and build a hand-and-foot-powered bicycle prototype – which worked! Volunteered to be the president of the International Human Powered Vehicle Association, an association of vehicle inventors. I coproduced the annual Human Powered Vehicle Speed Championships at the Indianapolis Motor Speedway in

1982, and established the DuPont Prize for Human Powered Speed (65 mph on a streamlined single-rider vehicle).

* Served as a corporate communications executive at Epson America, producing a U.S. video teleconference of Epson computer users in 1985. Then joined Walt Disney Imagineering followed by Disney Consumer Products. I was captivated and inspired by the creative energy at the Disney Company, its excellent production values and the company's rapid deployment of film, television, theme parks and consumer products.

* Worked with Disney artist Richard Duerrstein, who explained about the Disney magical sparkles or "pixie dust" that accompany the arrival of the Fairy Godmother in "Cinderella." They are of a distinctive yet simple star-shaped design that I now call the Twinkle. Twinkles follow Tinkerbell as she flies above the Disneyland castle in the Disney film logo.

* I concluded my career with several communications roles in education – at the public school district in Pasadena, California, then at Pasadena City College, and finally at the Office of Admissions at the University of California, Santa Barbara (No. 8 public university in the nation). There I deepened my fascination with academic subjects and teaching, which I hope can be enhanced with a focus on the Twinkle system of concept expression and organization.

More important here than the facts of my wandering life is the demonstration of "the Twinkle in action," which, as I say, can be a very direct route to successful writing.

Sometimes there is no Twinkle. All that I perceive is a word, possibly followed by many others. The software program Microsoft Word even offers the "outline format," which is a stepping back to the moments of inspiration.

In the outline process, or on the sidewalk of my life, there are a million other doorways, each one a day or a minute or a memory, each of which can be described as a single word and then a paragraph, or an essay, or a book, a video, a safe deposit box and on and on. Simply put, Twinkles are placeholders for a lot of news.

These Twinkles do *flit* as well – at the speed of thought, like the flash of sparklers. Each one could be an object, labeled and defined, moment or a thought, as fast as they may occur, like raindrops even. Catch them as you can.

Thinkers About Molecules

Ted Sargent, college professor and nanotechnologist, in his book "The Dance of Molecules," writes in considerable detail about new molecules in the process of being invented. My personal favorite concept among the many projects he cites, is the molecule-sized microcomputer known as a "Mote."

Sargent writes that "Motes," aka "smart dust," co-developed by UC Berkeley and the computer chip maker Intel, "are miniature self-contained battery-powered computers that use wireless links to exchange information. One day, thousands of these millimeter-size computers could be thrown into a field or a sensitive environmental area, forming a completely connected network of sensors."

Motes, Sargent writes, can "sense one another's presence and form their own ad hoc networks. Engineers have developed an operating system called TinyOS, to allow programs to run over the motes." (Page 108)

This is just one of many examples of new developments that may emerge from the scientific world of nanotechnology. Sargent is also interested in the concept of "bio-mimetics" where science studies life for secrets of its materials, such as the incredible stickiness of a gecko's grip on glass, or the phenomenal strength of a spider's strand of silk, and the rigidity of abalone shells made of calcium carbonate crystals.

His statement of process: "First, learn Nature's methods, then persuade her to manufacture new materials from the bottom up."

Nor does he think that such inventions should reside only in the world of the physical:

"Must the molecular and information views of the world stand opposed to one another? Not at all – nor indeed can they. As with light and electrons in networks, literalism and metaphor in prose, experiment and theory in science, rigor and creativity in all disciplines, true command over our parallel universes – the conceptual and the tangible – will be gained only once we see and harness their complementarity. For the dance of molecules to be anything other than a mosh pit, we need inspired choreography." ("Dance of the Molecules," Page 108)

The inspiring and productive career of inventor and futurist Buckminster Fuller is another compelling example of "thinking like a molecule." The conceiver of the geodesic dome and the streamlined, three-wheeled "dymaxion" car, clearly stated his intention to examine Nature for clues and to derive inventions to benefit all mankind.

In his 1981 Book, "Critical Path," Fuller said:

"Above all, I sought to comprehend the principles of eternally regenerative Universe, and to discover human functioning therein, thereby to discover nature's governing complexes of generalized principles and to employ these principles in the development of specific artifacts that would benefit humanity's fulfillment of its essential functioning in the cosmic scheme."

Fuller was captivated by the notion that structures in nature are built with "tensegrity," meaning that they assemble into forms not of heavy, solid materials like castle walls, but rather lightweight networks of continuous tension, interspersed with spar-like elements that allow for compression and resistance. The resulting shapes of molecules and soap bubbles, trees, animals and people exist in a perfect balance of tension and compression. Forces of pulling in and pushing away arrive at a compromise resolution that can remain stable.

On a larger scale, the moon is in perfect balance in its orbit around the earth. It falls toward the earth because of the gravitational attraction between the two, but its forward motion sends it "over the edge" of the earth at just the right speed, so that it never gets closer.

Ssimilarly, the two hydrogen atoms in a water molecule are each drawn to the oxygen atom, but are slightly repelled from each other (because they have the same positive electric charge). As a result, the three remain in a V shape, though the hydrogen atoms as a pair slip around and about the oxygen atom. Meanwhile, this threesome attaches lightly to other water molecules. And the infinite collection of H_2O atoms that collectively make water can lightly or strongly hold on to other materials that float in it. The ocean is rich in suspended salts and minerals, including gold, and *sugar* as my mother inspired me to know.

All molecules are assembled by these natural forces, which keep their atoms spaced together in unique arrangements that have their own integrity.

Fuller wrote further in "Critical Path":

"In 1927, I reasoned that if humans' experiences gave them insights into what nature's main objectives might be, and if humans committed themselves, their lifetimes, and even their dependents and all their assets toward direct, efficient, and expeditious realization of any of nature's comprehensive evolutionary objectives, nature might realistically support such a commitment."

With that rationale, Fuller decided to conduct his life as an "experiment," to see if by working in concert with nature's goals for human and earthly survival, his life would be supported, as if Nature or the Universe might actually provide some "wherewithal" to help advance his work.

"Acting entirely on my own initiative," he wrote, "I sought to discover what, if anything, can be effectively accomplished by a penniless, unknown individual, operating only on behalf of all humanity."

Whether or not Nature was the agent that offered him support, Buckminster Fuller found that his energetic experiment and his enthusiasm for mankind's potential survival and prosperity generated the income he hoped for. Also he did contribute "humanly favorable artifact development" (as he called it) in the form of new ideas for architecture and building, transportation, sanitation, maps and more.

In working on the geodesic dome, Fuller's key insight was that the forces of nature that can create a perfect soap bubble can also be used to build a beautiful building that uses a minimum of material to enclose a maximum amount of space.

The rules that he identified from nature are ones that we humans – as far as we know the chief exercisers of mind in the universe – should emulate and put to use on our own projects. Fuller said, "Don't fight forces; use them!" – a good way to start thinking like a molecule!

Fuller's daughter, Allegra Fuller Snyder, adds to the appreciation of her father with an article she published on the website of the Buckminster Fuller Institute. She attended the Dalton School in New York, which she says was devoted to "learning by doing."

"I don't think one can really confront Bucky's work without turning to the resource of one's own experiences, and the willingness to use those experiences as a basis for understanding. Understanding is an experiential word, particularly used in this context, with its sense of actually 'standing' physically 'under' an idea and experientially supporting the concept."

One other dramatic memorial to Bucky Fuller came in 1999 with the discovery of a molecular structure formed by 60 carbon atoms that organize themselves in nature into a perfect geodesic sphere: The formal name of the molecule is Buckminsterfullereen, but it's known more commonly today as the Buckyball.

As Ted Sargent wrote: "Scientist Harry Kroto said, on positing that the Buckyball, the European standard soccer ball, and Fuller's geodesic dome were all the same shape,

'It was so beautiful it just had to be right.'" (Dance of the Molecules, Page 22)

And another thinker about molecules is Janine M. Benyus, a writer and biologist who in her book, "Biomimicry: Innovation Inspired by Nature," documented many teams of scientists seeking to understand and emulate nature's building secrets – the strength and flexibility of a spider's silk for example. Her book pays great tribute to the scientists trying so assiduously to unravel the ways nature accomplishes her chemistries and systems design.

Thinking In Molecules

Thinking about the world at the level of molecules has made physics and chemistry valid and effective sciences for hundreds of years, and has brought us tremendous advances in comfort and well-being.

For Buckminster Fuller, thinking about the forces of Nature led to a new architectural shape: the geodesic dome, a highly efficient use of space and materials. By understanding those forces and assemblies, we understand much better the worldly bed we lie in, and are well poised to build better beds!

Such fresh, liberated and aware thinking by more people may possibly foster respect for our successes, increase admiration for learning, and for the vast potential of the human mind -- every mind.

Our visual imaginations are what provide this understanding of place and scale. Only in our imagination can we see the Universe's dimensions of large and small together as a total assemblage (which in truth may be at the edge of what many of us can actually imagine, even as we easily visualize gods and global warming!).

Flying in an airplane is another attractive way to grasp these large and small perspectives. From an altitude of 40,000 feet, a car on a highway looks like a tiny grain of sand (in which a whole world can reside, said the poet William Blake). With our powers of visual imagination, we can imagine ourselves sitting in our own cars below, warm and soothed by the radio. (Of course, projecting ourselves into a car on that road, we still won't be imagining exactly what it would be like to gaze out the window of that car, which serves as another introduction to the important topic of uncertainty.)

Personally, I enjoy imagining real places across those kinds of distances – landing on the moon or Pluto, or guessing what's going on inside of a glass of water, even contemplating something as familiar as coffee being ground and water passing through it to draw out the smallest grains. I think we all feel amazement at the powers that exist in very small spaces – the sperm, or the ovum for example, where so much information is packed into the DNA that resides in every one of our cells – the blueprints for our bodies!

I recall the 1936 science fiction short story "He Who Shrank," by Henry Hasse, about a scientist's assistant who

THINK LIKE A MOLECULE

drank a potion causing him to shrink in size, smaller and smaller. He floated down into universes that the author imagined might exist inside our own with sub-atomic planets orbiting atomic suns. He met some of the people on these new worlds inside our world. It was a mind-bending story.

Today, physicists have their atomic and molecular models fairly well figured out with their quantum mechanical calculations, the Higgs Boson, quarks and spin. However, it's no longer accepted to describe an atom with electrons orbiting the nucleus like the moon around the earth – because it's apparently not like that at all. Thinking about matter at the smallest scale is a complicated proposition. It suggests "fuzzy logic" and requires the embrace of uncertainty, as measured by statistics to estimate in what regions around a nucleus a particle might likely be found at any moment.

When you try to look at an electron or other fundamental atomic particle, you find it is something between a solid and a fuzzy wave packet, depending how you measure. That's the world of quantum mechanics.

Irfan Siddiqi, a professor of physics at UC Berkeley, wrote in an introduction to a lecture:

> "In the quantum world, an object can simultaneously exist in multiple states, the 'dead' and 'alive' condition of Schrödinger's cat being a quintessential example. It is the act of measurement that drives such a 'superposition' (simultaneous existences) to a more familiar classical outcome – 'dead' or 'alive' for the cat – thus bridging the gap between quantum

mechanics and our concept of reality. The precise nature of this 'wave function collapse' [deciding which state will be revealed] remains a topic of debate at the intersection of physics, mathematics, and philosophy. Recent experiments have reconstructed the real-time collapse of the wave function describing a two-state system, thereby filling in the details of this mysterious process."

The challenge for visualization is that, while the mathematics says that these sub-atomic particles may exist simultaneously in two different states, it's difficult for humans, with no direct visual references, to create meaningful mental pictures of what it would be like.

Science writer Meinard Kuhlmann in Scientific American magazine (August, 2013) wrote that current thinking in physics cannot say clearly what we should "see" at the smallest scale of electrons and quarks. For example, quantum theory seems to prove – at least the probability is not zero – that tiny energy packets (quanta) from a simple object like a coffee cup might be able to exist far away from where the object actually seems to be located.

Now that the insides of atoms are being explored and calculated to the smallest degrees of scale, it's getting harder to imagine what particles could be capable of such magical-seeming leaps, such an ephemeral existence. It's important to remember, however, that the picture we have of this sort of phenomenon is really a statistical calculation and not an actual observation. We are trying to visualize what the mathematics is asking us to imagine.)

Kuhlmann wrote in Scientific American, "If the mental images conjured up by the words 'particle' and 'field' (two ways of describing particles) do not match what the theory says, physicists and philosophers must figure out what to put in their place."

Animated films and many other efforts in graphical representation (especially using computer graphics allied with mathematical descriptions) have gone a long way to help us see the lively micro world that is undulating, jostling and shifting shapes all around us. (Also, check out the web site "Fold It," from the University of Washington. The professors and scientists invite gamers and anyone else who's interested to play at folding together protein molecules from the raw strands of amino acids that the DNA in effect turns into.

The fact is that molecules and the elements cling together dynamically in electric or magnetic bonds and float in the air or evaporate into the sunlight. Scientists often help animators draw such a scene, to help everyone visualize the molecular action. But in truth, any visual representation is an approximation; light waves are simply too blunt to capture the true look of a molecule. Besides, the look of a molecule may be downright fuzzy anyway, like a dust bunny hiding under a bed.

So, again, a molecule for us really is imaginary, a concept, an idea.

At the same time, molecules are old friends – like "H_2O equals Water." Two atoms of hydrogen, one of oxygen; NaCl is salt, and so on. When you start to understand chemistry, you begin to feel these assemblies. And yet, even for the pros, basically it's all an abstraction.

Note, that this is the point when we make the transition from our minds picturing the "real world," to our minds picturing a hypothetical world, just as a concept such as 2 plus 2 equals 4 is simultaneously an abstraction, and the real world.

It is amazing and wonderful that our species has the mental capacity to imagine different degrees of scale, from the atom to the distant galaxies. Moreover, understanding the "rules" such as mathematics that show the regularity and predictability of these molecular and/or planetary arrangements, also enables an exciting form of visualization. The rules, as Sir Isaac Newton found, are manifest in the natural motion of the pieces.

As another amusing example of real versus abstraction: we know how a chess knight moves according to the rules of chess – two squares up and one square over. But beyond an atom or a dust mote, a man-made chess knight can operate far beyond the rules of material order – he could even be a character in a television comedy show!

Action in the Abstract

So we are getting closer to our main purpose which is to raise the quality of our thinking through the use of new tools, and to create a new bridge between the worlds of the real versus the abstract or imaginary.

While a molecule may not think, atoms and molecules do perform "actions." They are the very first level of action in our universe (after the Big Bang). Atoms and molecules assemble naturally, all on their own, into diamonds, water and trees; whales, suns, people and planets.

These molecular powers are not "intentional," but simply part of the physical characteristics of the materials; the "powers" are merely the influence they bring to their environments, their innate capability to react and combine, leading to cascading systems of events.

Such cause and effect relationships were humorously celebrated by the artist and cartoonist Rube Goldberg as seen in the elaborate, machine-like systems he presented in his drawings. The interlinking "processes" showed events, like a dog scratching his flea, knocking over a glass that spills water into a plant, which grows and pushes a lamp switch. His progression of cause-and-effects leading to new causes illustrated, in humorous style, the way change often happens in nature.

Our universe is like a giant erector set of Legos and Tinkertoys, parts fitting together in so many ways. We humans have the ability to see those assemblies, to understand how the pieces fit together, and as a result we can design other systems that fit together well.

When I stand in my garage, surrounded by tools and "high-potential junk," it is fun to find that the added element I need on the latest project is lying in a drawer to the left. In the same way, people assemble into an infinity of arrangements such as families, tribes, business organizations and nations. These assemblies are generally defined by rules and mental intentions (both conscious and not). People collect at the beach on a sunny day, or seat themselves in rows at a football game. Based on a complex set of rules that are somewhat analogous to natural forces, these social structures will be stable, fluid, or even volatile. Sometimes a crowd at a soccer game will explode!

Humans and other animals naturally assemble in social arrangements – ants or bees in their colonies, wolves in their packs, and fish in their schools. Sometimes the arrangements are even amusing to notice. Birds may line up on telephone wires like musical notes on a staff. And guests at a cocktail party will maintain socially accepted distances according to rules they barely notice, but which nonetheless cause the grouping to take on various shapes and motions, including hugs of greeting, or awkward moves of avoidance.

Every one of these shapes and arrangements has integrity – or "tensegrity" as Bucky Fuller expressed it – based on the resolution of forces at play.

In the same way, "thinking like a molecule" is being aware of the context in which you live; of the forces and influences that you manifest, of the influences that bear upon you. Also like a molecule, you have natural energy (stored and kinetic), electrical currents, pushing and pulling motion, forward propulsion and attitude. The critical difference for you and me in the world: we also have *purpose* and *intention*. We are in the world, ready and moving ahead to react and engage according to our nature and ideas. And, you and I can do more than merely react; we can proactively engage (something that Raskolnikov thought about a lot in Dostoyevsky's novel "Crime and Punishment").

How far down in the orders of life does such thought-directed action occur? The first emergent forms of life did not automatically engage in thinking, did they? Isn't "thinking" for the higher orders that emerged later, such as professors and rocket scientists? Which animals can think? Whales and porpoises? Monkeys and bonobos? Lizards and worms?

Clearly some form of thinking or intention motivates a worm to dig its way out of soil that is waterlogged from the rain. But, something *other* than thinking provokes a match to burst into flame when it is scraped on the side of a matchbox. That's straight cause and effect. But, thinking certainly involves some cause-and-effect relationship as one idea reacts to, or is ignited by, another.

In the book, "The Way of the Cell," microbiologist Franklin M. Harold ponders the living, acting life "force" that emerges from the molecular and chemical components of the common microscopic, single-celled organism *Eshirichia coli.*

"I share the commitment to a material conception of life," Harold writes, "but that makes it doubly necessary to remember that before the cells were taken apart—as long, indeed, as they were alive—they displayed capacities that go beyond chemistry.... How do millions, even billions of molecules come to function in a collective, purposeful mode?"

That's my question, too. We may not answer it here, but I cannot stop marveling at the idea of it.

Out of its natural forces and molecular relationships, our physical world has somehow fostered action-related thinking, imagination and creativity. As a result, birds can build nests and fly the same migration routes they have flown for millennia. People can build cars and roads, and write books about their travels. These sometimes instinctive, sometimes planned and intentional actions, seem to arise naturally from, or "supervene" (compare "intervene") on the physical elements of the biological systems.

As a dog owner, I can clearly see that thinking of some sort is going on in my puppy's head. It's not verbalized, but Petey the dog is clearly studying clues about what I'm likely to do, whether I may offer a treat, set out for a walk, or just settle down for quiet time.

The important idea for me is that, to get to the root causes of thinking, we need to admit that somewhere in our molecules and cells there is representation going on, capturing images or ideas of the world outside. Personally, my theory is that consciousness arises when one "thought" in the mind triggers another, and that perhaps triggers two more – and this constant moving wave of thought vs counter thought, flashing forward and upward is ultimately "consciousness."

Our tools, of course, make a tremendous difference in seeing the world in more detail, and in focusing our consciousness, especially using the pencil, paintbrush, tape recorder, camera, and so on.

Development of the telescope helped Galileo learn that Jupiter has moons. Even today, people may be surprised to peer through a telescope and see those tiny moon-dots – Io, Europa, Calisto, Ganymede and the 59 other moons – so far from us, yet so clearly in relationship with the giant planet. Now we are "conscious" of those moons, and how far away are the stars.

With spacecraft sending signals back to earth (from Pluto, for example), followed up by TV news, magazine articles, cameras and websites, we have gained quite a clear idea of what our solar system's planets and moons look like. We have effectively stood on the surface of Mars and peered through the rings of Saturn. We have "been there," thanks to our tools.

Dutch scientist Antonie van Leeuwenhoek is famous as one of the first people (1674) to point a microscope at a cilia-waving protozoan commonly found in roadside water culverts. The microscope and even more powerful tools today make it ever clearer how amazingly interwoven and functionally complex is the miniature world the creatures inhabit.

As we watch these microorganisms, it's hard not to wonder how much they are aware of their surroundings. In fact, that single-celled swimmer "knows" when some food is near, and tries to avoid unpleasant environments, perhaps by sensing the molecular "smell" of key chemicals. Looking into the eyepiece of a microscope, it's easy to wonder just what that elementary form of life does feel or think.

Happily, we have these tools to project us into these different dimensions and help us appreciate the new perspectives.

A Mirror On the Micro World

In the next section of this book, I will delve more into the new "tool," the Twinkle, which serves to help us notice moments of dawning awareness, to recognize when our minds are expanding.

I respond to the ideas of science the way many do who heard Carl Sagan talk about "billions and billions" of stars, or who read Francis Crick and James D. Watson explain how they figured out the structure of DNA. The universe is a stimulating place, and it's fun to think about it.

I contend, again, that it's useful to picture ourselves as elements or functioning pieces in the world, like molecules. We are not just small; that's not the point. But like molecules, we are endowed with energy and innate capabilities unique to each of us and our own history. We combine with other people in bonds of friendship or need. In our world, things that interest us and influence us go around and come around again, like chance encounters with high school friends or viewing a flash of lightning. These processes all mirror the micro world.

A molecule – which may help break down a sugar, or aid in locating the atom of potassium it needs to finish making a human cell – is successful because it's in the right place at the right time. As the saying goes, "What goes around, comes around." As the beginning, the right elements happened to be in the right place when the lightning struck; so life began. Being embedded in the total environment helps us gather the right pieces when we need them – molecules of oxygen when we breathe, or the way a female ovum may experience a flood of spermatozoa at just the right time of the month.

Occasionally even accidents create progress. A DNA molecule may be mutated by a random cosmic ray, and perhaps a proto-eyeball is born, ready to evolve over billions of years. But a lot of life and biology is predicated on the idea that the continuous presence of something in the environment makes possible following interactions that come to depend on its presence.

One reason that evolution has worked over the millions of years is that changes in an individual's DNA, which might actually help the organism survive, are preserved in the DNA of later generations to help them survive as well, and their offspring, too. Success breeds more success.

Thinking like a molecule means that we are more aware of the fundamental rules that support atoms, molecules and people in their lives, and in their process of building the universe. That's what we as people are about – in our case also adding of a lot of effective and potentially positive thinking power.

I am not trying to reduce our thinking to a clockwork model of the universe, where all is known and predictable. In fact, I invite us to a place where final answers may never be known. Uncertainty has to be embraced. That's the way it is at the smallest level, the absolutely small dimension of all matter.

Also, taking a molecular view, complete with an awareness of chance, uncertainty and the unknown, but also noting possible new compounds and structures, new possibilities, leads us metaphorically to a new awareness and respect for our individual and collective subconscious, wherein lies our potential to create new ideas. Each subconscious mind is like a person's personal volcano, ready at any moment to spurt hot new world-building material from the depths.

Some writers have proposed that the number of possible connections or ideas latent amid our many billions of brain cells is greater in number than all the stars in the universe – in one single mind!

It's a lovely thought if a statement such as that is accurate. Most likely, the potential for good in our human species *is* infinite. That should be a source of hope and ambition towards better living for all. It's with that sense of awe and empowerment that this book is written.

A Question of Perspective . . .

The average person may not frequently consider just how big *and* how small we are in the wide scheme of things. (The mind-bending short film, "Powers of 10," by Charles and Ray Eames, available on YouTube, is a lively "adventure in magnitudes," as the description goes. I recommend to everyone!) However, our minds do comprehend in a general way what's going on. We know we are "big," and we know we are "small." We even know, roughly, the limits to what we know. We all can create a picture of the Big Bang, though it's difficult to imagine anything "before" that event. In fact, there may not actually have *been* anything "before" the Big Bang event. Not even time existed before the Big Bang, which limits our ability to imagine what might have come before.

How will the Universe end? What is dark matter? What is an atom or a molecule, exactly? We all have to face the fact – there is much we do not or cannot know.

Despite the limits to our knowledge and our imagination, we have actually grown a lot in our understanding about the universe in which we live. This book is an invitation to join the party of awareness and understanding, and to participate in the gains – mental and physical – that such visions afford.

However, as I have said, the universe is not reducible to certainties. This book invites you to consider that our Universe may never reveal final answers. Get comfortable with uncertainty. (Fortunately, both in our planning for the "real world," and in our knowledge of the atomic world, we already embrace uncertainty, and we plan for it. Witness "make-up dates in case of rain.")

The important idea for me is that we billions of human beings are obviously capable of magnificent acts of positive creation – as witnessed by the continuous explosion in recent years of new technologies, better farming methods, worldwide transportation and communication marvels, space travel and life-prolonging medicine, vast powers of computer calculation, simulation and prediction – so much. By focusing our powers of inspiration, we can do even more – though controlling our animalistic enmities and instincts needs to be part of the mental miracle!

Our knowledge of what is going on at the ends of the universe, and down to the smallest scale of atoms and quarks, stretches human imagining to the maximum. So, of course, does trying to guess exactly what someone else might be thinking!

Theorists in atomic structure have identified fundamental particles using sophisticated mathematical reasoning, but right now there is not a descriptive visualization that mere mortals can understand.

It's a worthy effort, but lest I look silly trying, creating vivid new images of molecules that are consistent with quantum theory is not my goal in writing this book. The question is open, and so is the question of our ultimate fate. For now, I am willing to embrace the uncertainty, and to take it on faith that clarity may one day emerge. Our understandings will continue to evolve, just as we have learned what a tiny place earth really is, and just as we – hopefully – will learn to guide ourselves through the uncertain future.

Taking the molecular view with an awareness of serendipity and the vast potential of the unknown – what does lie in the next galaxy? – leads us metaphorically to a new awareness and respect for our individual and collective subconscious and our pure potential to create new ideas, original formulations, just like the alchemists of old, or the chemical and biological engineers of today.

We can be excited again about the number of ideas that can be created among those brain cells. To say it again: the potential for positive, adaptive innovation in our species is vast.

With this potential in the physical human mind, our fantastic brains almost seem to exist to provide a "voice" for the universe. Through exploration of the natural world, our intentional minds seek to provide intelligence and awareness for nature itself – where there had never been a previous moment in Nature of "expressed intention," except in the palpable but wordless will to survive and breed. (This is a question that God or the aliens will help us resolve one day.)

By contrast, "thinking like a molecule" means feeling the intense awareness that nature's events – such as the breeze in the field at night and rain in the morning – are indeed happening all on their own, with no perceptible mind to cause or explain events. Events just are, but *we* are thought-full observers.

Thinking like a molecule is being in a Zen state of mind, with a fuller appreciation of the natural activity of the universe. We search for the presence of a higher power for the simple reason that we want an explanation, dialog with another mind that might know more of what's going on, that perhaps has made all this happen on purpose, some entity that knows something of how it all came to be. If only we could meet some larger mind that knows the answers, that sees the larger view, has a clue, and can explain it all to us.

Well, for now I believe we have met that source of wisdom and intelligence, and it is us!

When we think like a molecule, we are entering our universe at a new level of comprehension and sense of responsibility. We are closer to understanding the calculations of chance and effective association (e.g. contracts in support of positive cooperative action). I hope that the mental exercise of envisioning this role for ourselves, coupled with a willingness to make space for uncertainty, readies us to appreciate our living world and bestows a new readiness to live peacefully and fruitfully, thanks to the insights.

By touring the "imaginary" world of molecules, we become visitors more empowered in the world of ideas, of potential innovations, with a broader understanding of the universe – rising up from our earthbound perspective as animals limited by gravity, air, sunrise and moonrise, the rhythms and forces of daily life. With mind and language, we can journey with new vision and hope, limited only by our willingness, courage, and intention to live better.

2

THE TWINKLE - A MOLECULE
OF MEANING

In this second part of "Think Like a Molecule," I want to focus on the idea of the Twinkle, a new use of the word, as "a molecule of meaning."

I hope I have been clear that for me (and for Buckminster Fuller and Ted Sargent), there exists "structure beneath our structure." Our minds are contained and function within the supporting system of our bodies. Bridges stand using strong girders and taut cables. Also, beyond the visible, there are structures formed by atoms and molecules such as the fluid dynamics of water and the life giving helical form of DNA.

As Fuller wrote with Robert Marks in "The Dymaxion World of Buckminster Fuller": "Men do not make structures out of 'materials'; they make large structures out of small structures.... The limits of the visible spectrum do not represent the threshold of change between man-devised structures and nature-devised structures." (Page 40)

I add to the discussion: there are structures in the realm of pure thought – expressed representations of intangible ideation. These include the written word and visual artwork, construction plans and designs, film scripts and stories, all depicting imagination arriving in the real world. These idea structures are often constructed by the writer, but also by the artist, architect, draftsman, engineer, composer, business planner, lawyer – you get the idea.

In this book, I present the idea of the Twinkle as a way to recognize and mark the moment when a thought occurs – when something that is intangible yet real and possibly world-changing – "an idea" – can spring into existence as an almost magical addition to the Universe.

Original thoughts are like elevators arriving from the subconscious. The door slides opens and a thought appears. Sometimes, the thought happens, then we *realize* it has come, and consider what it means to have such a thought – what should I do about it?

There are many parts to the magic of ideation: language to describe it, perhaps in book length form (with countless Twinkles involved); history, seeing the context of such a thought; and even science and literature to help us understand and communicate our thoughts.

Such apparently spontaneous creation is not quite "something for nothing." It does require the energetic presence of Life, and the structure upon structure of the subconscious functioning of brain cells to produce what might look like "original thought." And, it does depend how you define "original." Tom Sawyer never existed until Mark Twain thought of him, but it took a lot of experience in the life of Samuel Clemens to create that original story.

How deeply in the brain does a new thought reside? How dependent is action on thought? What categories can help define "thought"? These are questions that can be answered many ways, weighed on sliding scales. Some individuals are capable of sleepwalking and talking, with no idea that they are doing it. Somewhere, consciousness enters into the discussion of thought.

In my mind, noticing a Twinkle is the essence, or the first step of "meta-cognition." It's when I identify, view, reflect on, and ultimately record my thoughts. The purpose of a Twinkle is to mark a first moment of thought, before a word has formed. It's the moment that one becomes aware that a new thought has arrived. It's a tool to symbolize and represent thought itself. After that – even a fraction of a second later – the thought is named. (I call the central point the "Define"). Then the thought can be analyzed, evaluated, expanded upon, written down, and so on. Thus, a Twinkle is a geometrical, geographical canvas ready to record the thought that has been noticed by the thinker.

No other person has any real hope of knowing exactly when a thought occurs to anyone, or what the thought might be. Perhaps an observer will see a troubled look flit across the face of a miscreant, or a there will be a "eureka" expression when a brilliant solution comes to mind. But only the thinker has any ability to describe thoughts in detail.

The progression is as follows: One can mark the arrival of a thought with something like a Twinkle or a lightbulb. Next, it can be restated to oneself in words or an image. Then perhaps a note or image may be transcribed onto paper or the thinker says to the next person, or into a tape recorder: "You know what . . . ?"

The dissecting and parsing of thoughts, then writing them down, is a most twinkling sort of process. A dot of ink from a pen is in contact with a piece of paper. Then, the dot/twinkle begins to move, creating a line to represent letters or an image.

The Twinkle is like a physics of thought, a molecule of meaning. The fanciful unit of "thought architecture" provides a structure with the flexibility to locate and define molecules (picture one million atoms across a single strand of hair), and to define the birth and growth of ideas.

At the same time, a Twinkle provides space to express that idea and the infinite potential the idea may hold. Any question you ask about the Twinkle concept can be answered and added to the Twinkle structure, Wikipedia style.

With the concept of the Twinkle, I hope to represent the limitless nature of mind to comprehend the universe from beginning to end, and to improve the world, as Bucky Fuller did. Twinkles also serve as tool sets to develop molecular ideas, and other constructions physical and imaginary.

The twinkle is a particular way to "draw meaning" and connect concepts in space for understanding and comparison. This conceptual "geography of meaning" is proposed as a way to represent any number of ideas and physical things including individuals, organizations, places, relationships, the marking and passage of time, a larger concept of "location," religion, and even a way to think of The Big Bang.

The Basic Drawing

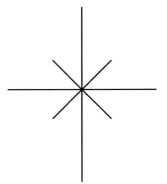

In a key scene from the Disney film, "Cinderella," the Fairy Godmother arrives to turn mice into horses, and a pumpkin into a coach so Cinderella can attend the ball after all. The Fairy Godmother appears at the moment when Cinderella is crying and feeling hopeless that her dreams are dashed. In the emotional stillness, we first see an emerging and enlarging group of twinkling stars that Disney animators created, which later became virtually a Disney trademark.

Former Disney artist Richard Duerrstein described the Disney stars – Twinkles is my name for them – as part of the Disney company legacy. The Disney star is a simple and obvious design, which may in fact harken to early religious drawings. A vertical member is tall; that and the horizontal crossbeam intersect at their midpoints; then two shorter lines cross through the center point, each at 45 degrees to the first two. Multiple Twinkles or stars of various sizes placed in a group suggest depth of space. In the Disney animated films and Disney lore, a sprinkling of the stars is called pixie dust.

In that scene from "Cinderella," the Twinkles (especially in that romantic, fairy tale context) represent myriad possibilities coming forth magically from nowhere, a complete change in the environment, a paradigm shift, a "pixilation of space," seeming to enable an opening into another universe. It stands for magic! It's the symbol that mice can turn into horses, and a pumpkin can become a glittering royal carriage. Imagination is realized.

This is an essential part and purpose of the Twinkle – to be a placeholder for the imagination, onto which an infinite number of possible and actual meanings can be placed.

The essence of the basic Twinkle drawing is that multiple lines intersect at a point. Conventional x, y and z axes invented by Rene Descartes in the mid-1600s, can be joined by many other lines, generally through the central point. Moreover, the lines are dynamic – possibly moving, sliding, turning on and off, and reflecting light like glass or chrome. The mind and eye go to this twinkling image as to street lights against a dark mountain side.

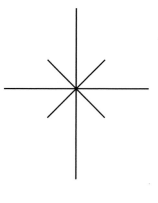

In constructing the Twinkle shape, we give the central "zero" point a definition or meaning – a "Define" – such as a word, a general or specific person, a city, a country, an organization, some idea, even a generalized intuition. The many lines that can go through the central point – an infinite number of lines – can be aspects or dimensions of a highly complex core idea – for example, "a multi-faceted person," or perhaps more precisely a "multi-lineated" person. The lines can all represent aspects of the central point or idea – size, character, population, and so on.

So there is the first basic shape: a "Twinkle" representing virtually any "meaning" (as defined at the central point), to which we'd like to assign descriptive attributes (lines).

The "First Value" of the Basic Drawing is that it can encompass many lines/ideas/attributes of a (so far) single yet possibly highly complex idea (person, city, concept, fairy princess, etc.).

A second value of the Basic Drawing is that it incorporates the concept of "interruption," an issue in life and in thought. The Y axis meets the X axis at a point where – usually – both lines have the value of zero.

As in basic Euclidian geometry, but also incorporating "Cartesian coordinates" as invented by Rene Descartes in the 1600's, the X axis has zero as a "start" (or one should perhaps say "negative infinity as a start" at the far left end of the X line). A counting or hashing of the line can indicate changing values of, say, distance or time passing, increasing speed, and so on. In each case, the line is interrupted by any number of data points. (Sometimes for "lines" I also say "data spars.")

A third value of the basic Twinkle drawing is that it does not need to be precisely defined to have some utility. I can say that "he's highly excitable," or "she's very rich," and a version of a basic Twinkle drawing may feel quite suitable to that description. The point is that we can assign a Twinkle as a placeholder to the vaguest intuition. Then the idea can, if needed, be developed more fully, perhaps as a simple writing exercise. The lines that make up and "explain" the Twinkle may turn into the bullet points of an essay outline, which subsequently is massaged into a finished piece of writing, or into a painting or a technical drawing. Something that started as a pure intuition, an idea without words, can make its way – grow into – a fully articulated argument or explanation.

It's possible that ultimately an observer could look at a Twinkle that is intended merely to convey a vague intuition, and learn something from it without reading a separate description first – the way we can very quickly read emotions in a face, for instance when we see a smile or a frown. The "Unified Feel Theory" (I jokingly call it) suggests that perhaps one day the feelings or intuition of an observer could be represented or stimulated by the basic Twinkle shape, perhaps with color and animation. However, the way we learn to write with it, or read it in detail, is still to be determined. At this stage, it's the beginning of an alphabet without a complete language beyond our native tongues.)

More Basics

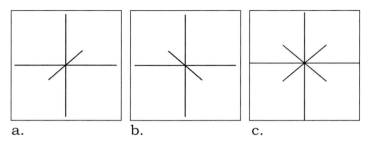

a.   b.   c.

When we look at these basic Twinkle shapes, and see one spar missing (figures a and b), our mind's eye understands that we are looking at the X,Y and Z axes. (I do assume that in any Twinkle, the X-Y-Z axes are there amid the countless other possible spars.) But in adding the fourth line (c), our eye is confused. We are no longer sure if it's three dimensions. In fact, the image is reduced to a flat plane of x and y, and other lines. If we *insist* on seeing it in three dimensions, then the second short line is either a random line in space that happens to go through the zero point, OR it's a crude representation of a line that's perpendicular to each of the other axes, therefore creating a Fourth Dimension. While that "could be" the case, that is hard to visualize, so for now my view is that I see another data spar in the three dimensional space. At the same time, every single data spar is a "dimension" of the Zero Point Idea, the Define, adding whatever additional meaning we conceive of.

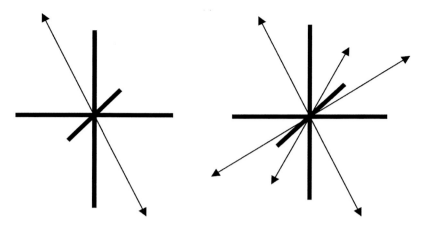

Here we see (in drawing A) that the three X, Y and Z axes now also have another data line in position, through the zero point. In drawing (B), right, we see that three data spars are now in place, so three additional dimensions or aspects of this concept are included (whatever the words or definitions of the data spars might be as related to the core idea or "Define").

Orienting Twinkles for the Quick Read

Which way is UP in a Twinkle?

Ultimately, we should be able to orient a Twinkle Shape up and down, left and right. Perhaps we could define what is the "up" of a basic shape. Assuming that a Twinkle might be free floating like a soap bubble, or rotating in space at any angle, orientation should be completely variable. However, by the conventions of mathematical terminology, the x axis is usually horizontal, the y axis is usually vertical, and z projects in front. However, that orientation can change.

If in fact a Twinkle were to be free-floating like a soap bubble, it could invert or spin. If a human head with a face were to do that, our mind's eye would quickly understand which view is up.

One possible orientation strategy would be analogous to the common practice of placing red and green lights on the left and right sides of a boat or airplane. In that case, the orientation of the airplane in space (e.g. coming at us or going away) can be understood with a glance, thanks to the lights.

At some point, an accessible universal concept (or concepts) could provide the sense of orientation for a Twinkle, to help us "read" its meaning at a glance. For instance, our ability to read faces is a talent that lies deep in our consciousness. Arms and legs and torsos provide further orientation for our brains. For our Twinkles, could there be a conceptual face, arms, legs, etc. to orient us to its meaning? Also, perhaps there is a fundamental set of descriptors of universal interest such as "danger," "important," "life sustaining," positive/negative emotion, or simple information. The possibility of instant orientation, enabling readers to decipher a Twinkle's meaning, would begin to tap these reading resources.

To pursue this further: Consider these orientation hierarchies:

Cold = Yin-analytical on top.

Warm-expressive-"human" on bottom?

Note: this color/temperature distribution is semi-analogous to the earth, outside to the inside – cooler on the outside, warmer and more animalistic at the private interior.

Other representational and "orientational" strategies will be sought. Also: seeing Twinkles in animated form, rotated on a computer screen, would help showcase the three-dimensional nature of this symbolic tool. Limited to the printed page, a fuller view is difficult.

Questions:

How can we ever "read" a shape that is so complex? Answer: Each spar or line of data can be compressed to a supremely tiny type size, labeled with a file name and storing associated text, and can be read out like any text file. A computer would be able to read all the lines of data very quickly. And yes, a Twinkle would be most intelligible in a computer screen or a hologram, where a cursor can touch upon the data spars more conveniently in a clear 3-D space.

Another option for a Twinkle would be a data file attached or referenced (possibly just one line of data) that lists all the associated words? Again, the lines may themselves be made of letters and words, formulas or mathematical functions that produce answers on a continuous basis. Each Twinkle is unique, but its core and structure is part of an infinite family.

Another question is: How does a line of data that touches the central point represent, for instance, a "population" (a changing but currently single number). How does it actually make a line? Isn't it just a "data point"? Or does the population number start at zero? Or is it a full discussion and analysis of each feature or characteristic of the Twinkle's "define" (primary label or definition).

Yes it does. But, is there any way to define a "negative" population?

There's a Twinkle concept for you. Perhaps we can think of a definition.

Sometimes lines do have value -- in the spread of a person's interest in jellybeans for instance. Sometimes "I love jellybeans" (longer line); sometimes I'm not interested in them at all, i.e. no line at all. Does the total length of a line represent the data? Then how would an "8 million" count for Los Angeles population be located on the "LA City Twinkle" population line? At 4 million? So plus four, minus a minus four: thus a net representation of 8 million? I don't think so. The population would grow from zero to 8 million, but what would be the "negative" population? Would that be . . . a potential population? The smaller the negative, the more likely a population? An uninhabited planet could have a small minus-negative (i.e. "more likely") population spar, population line.

(This all seems to border on the meaningless, but the point is that each Twinkle is infinite, so it can encompass all discussion about anything. "Monkeys: Start your typewriters!")

Can Twinkles intersect or combine, and is this useful, or comprehensible?

Yes, the Basic Shapes can interact in countless ways. Imagine lines of force in a magnet – bending toward the magnetic poles. (Twinkle lines are not necessarily straight. They may bend or intertwine.)

One last idea: A Twinkle can also develop or represent a full spherical image, like a globe of video, by simply producing a video screen at the end of a data spar, screens that could combine into larger, semi-spherical images, such as a face.

Twinkles in Motion

I enjoy imagining these shapes in rapid and dynamic motion, keeping full pace with my thoughts in rapid fire, as numerous and fast-moving as raindrops if need be, appearing and changing at the speed of thought. They may be floating in an array down the sidewalk, or flying and swirling like a flock of birds. They may be dancing around each other, defining a space near and far. All these spaceships of meaning are floating amid and among each other . . . and suddenly -- swoop -- there's a link which can then fade quickly, or grow brighter. The spars can align or connect; an entire array around a point can slide together with others or overlap and coalesce in three dimensions. In these imaginings, the Twinkles connect in the way of airline route maps, spider webs spread across the planet.

Lines projecting out of a "Define" (the zero-point core) can bend and connect with other Twinkles in an infinite number of ways (perhaps bending like lines of force in a magnet). The "live" ones strengthen as they connect; the unconnected ones may simply fade away or remain unconnected. Think also of the image of a cell in mitosis. As the nucleus divides into two nuclei, the chromosomes stretch between the two cells. Then the matter divides into two centers, two cells, and the membranes close around the now-separate two new cell bodies. Such motion and change is possible with this conceptual tool the Twinkle.

On a data line, there will be perhaps infinite numbers of interruptions or data recordings. Data lines representing variable measures such as weight or volume, data points can come anywhere, usually beginning with "hypothetical" – a placeholder for possible data to be gathered and organized.

A house can be another example of a Define of a Twinkle. During its lifetime, a house will witness people and animals, furniture and pictures coming in and out, each one another "data point," a historical event. Most of these changes are not recorded, but all of them are part of the history of the house, and each of these parts of the house's history can form the countless numbers of Twinkles that add up to form the "total Twinkle" of the house and its history, including the front door, the kitchen sink, the roof, visits, births, deaths – an infinity of "defines." This encyclopedic complex of Twinkles becomes a conceptual way of representing history. They collapse into one another as the total package. Or they can leap out again into separate groups of people, furniture, events, holidays, accidents, paint colors, ad infinitum.

This is also akin to the development of computer menus and windows that jump open with click of a mouse. A Twinkle almost seems a model of the basic neural cells that connect throughout our brains, all twinkling with the electro-chemical magic of our thoughts.

One central idea is that every event, object or person in time is waiting to be named according to when a mind sees the need. Ultimately, it is only in the naming that there can be a Twinkle or a data line, but the infinite nature of a

Twinkle suggests that the data lines are there, even before they are called out.

A Twinkle emerges in a moment of intuition, even if you can't put your finger on it yet. In that case, a name may be called for, and may soon be applied. Possibly it already was applied like a stake in the ground. The old grizzled prospector says, "I'll dig here someday, at this X on the map, and who knows <u>what</u> I'll find!"

Axiom: There is an infinity of possible data spars attached to any Define.

The Twinkle is a tool to describe concepts real or hypothetical. The shapes don't necessarily need to be defined right away.

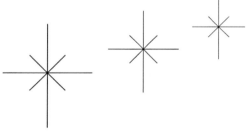

Initially, they are useful because they can represent an idea or physical thing very rapidly, even intuitively. In fact, the shape can represent an idea or a thing so rapidly partly because it says "Think of this shape as a placeholder for this concept – "love," or "Poughkeepsie NY" – and it doesn't yet *matter* precisely how it fits with the concept. Thinking about the shape merely says: "When you think about 'love,' we all know there are many, many aspects to that topic. Love is happiness. Love is my memory of mother."

As a starting point in considering an idea, you have a shape onto which you may place (or be inspired to consider) other aspects of the concept. But it's good to start by being aware that many aspects are possible and even likely. Open your mind. Start the accumulation of other ideas, dimensions and tangents. It's about being open to the many possible aspects of everything, everyone a line of "data," and "empirical" to some degree (at least in the abstract!). And merely having the vision of "many possible aspects" to consider, we are going in with an open mind. This happens in the very first thought – the shape representing "idea" or "define."

The rapidity with which these shapes can change can be breathtaking. Think *molecular* changes. Think of the rapidity of change seen in chemical reactions – millions or billions or more molecules interacting each second. Each chemical, theoretically, can be described with a Twinkle, detailed in data spars with its name, shape, ionic properties, and countless other factors.

We can even imagine that a Twinkle represents all the thoughts you have *right now*, and can change as quickly as your attention can change – now thinking of the game last night, now the road in front of the car as you drive, now the radio announcer, now the game again, NOW THAT KID in the street. The lines move in and out, change emphasis depending what your mind has turned to. Theoretically, the shapes show the range of ideas, meanings, etc., in your mind at any time, which can come instantly, and go away just as fast. In the event of a distraction, a new line can enter the Basic Drawing in a flash. You can spew Twinkles of thought and ideas and other intellectual placeholders all the time, the way bubbles might float out of the washing machine, the way a KO'd boxer is surrounded by stars.

Assumption: All things have many aspects and endless histories; it's helpful to be aware.

Data spars of a "Define" may or may not intersect the central zero point. They may relate to a number of other Define points.

Separately, data lines may have "data points" that are actually "data planes" (think of them as pictures) that are separated in time. These images may showcase, explain or represent moments in the life of a Define (or in the life of a series of defines, if a data line is associated and influenced by a number of separate define points).

Here is something of a change in the discussion of Defines. One Define may be summarized, perhaps, as several Define points represented or summarized in one point (e.g. a red-orange rose). But red, orange and rose are Defines with infinite numbers of "data spars" that go through the center point. Also, it could be a rose, orange-red.

An image comes to me around this concept of landing spaces -- a microscopic-telescopic view of a line coming up out of, or going down-into, a Define. As we'll see more clearly someday, these lines are so complicated and capable of such gymnastics that one must be careful to see them as not always simple. When we think of the idea of landing spaces, this relates to a line traveling in toward, or away from, a Define. (Note that the landing spaces or floor planes, or rooms built up from these floors, are moments in time that can capture or represent or embody some form or moment in the life of that Define (each define is dynamic and changing). It's very much the way that an animated film exists in the shape of 24 frames per second, each one a snapshot of events in time – or the way that a bullet can be captured in steps moving through the middle of an apple. One BIG step, a fuzzy blur of motion with many causes and effects inside of it (e.g. a black box), is actually an explanation of events over time, and not a simple representation of an event. (For example "When we see this phone booth, this is where Superman chose to change his clothes and emerged to confront the bad guy." That is, more may be going on than meets the eye.)

Ultimately, as we get more comfortable with these ideas, data lines may or may not go exactly through a Define. The Define may be "approximate." There may be another define somewhat close or very close, but we don't know exactly the word or words to separate them. This does relate very much to the sorts of ambivalence and confused anxiety that any person may experience, or that might also reflect an injured, sleepy or drunken state. (But I insist that some amount of twinkling focus of attention can exist – beyond which "consciousness" is no more.)

Out of a Define, or even out of "undefined defines," come several centers at once – perhaps an infinity of lines, moving and curving and "incoming" to a Define that may be different, the same, similar – so that an infinity of lines of force can curve through space and intersect each other, move through each other, coalesce and – this to me is the biggest idea – at some time in the future, all come together, every single "define" into a moment, perhaps like the Big Bang, when they are all perfectly aligned at the same moment (all the monkeys wrote the same lines of Shakespeare at once). At that moment, in essence, we lose consciousness because nothing is observing anything else, we are every one of us, in the perfect moment, without memory, because again we are all without any form of attention, all of our attention is devoted to the moment of perfection, there is nothing else. After that, all is Birth.

As my brother in law Charley would have said, "Wow, molecules man."

Imagining Twinkles

Today I imagined the Hollywood Hills as defined by Twinkles; so that later (thanks to huge computing power), every home and blade of grass and square inch of asphalt could be rolled forward like a dust storm coming across the plain.

Motion capture movies are using Twinkles in this way. Actors are decorated with dots on their faces, their bodies, arms and legs. As they move, the camera –catches their dots, then translates them to analogous dots on a drawn image – for example, the creature Gollum in "The Lord of the Rings" played by Andy Serkis. The motion of that moving actor was translated into very realistic motion in the animated figure.

Twinkles enable a leap from the imaginary world to the real world. Twinkles laid out first in the imagination transition onto lines on paper, which then perhaps become girders of a skyscraper rising above Manhattan.

Twinkle. A thought! A possibility! A light goes on. Out of the stillness, out of the silence and the unknown, comes thought, then being, and then awareness.

In the Beginning

Adam and Eve and our real primeval ancestors grew in their awareness, up from animal instinct, into awareness (or so we were taught in catechism school) of their shame at being naked. Then, a higher awareness still arrived, of being capable and hopeful. Their consciousness grew until today humans have enormous powers of self-awareness (thought still not sufficient self-control).

That self-awareness is a flood of Twinkles, notations of what it occurs to us today to do tomorrow, for example.

Think like a molecule -- just before the awareness we have of our own process.

Why? Because the natural world, the molecule, the forest, the system of a stream, the caress of the wind, all can express themselves– through our minds, our identified awareness.

Then, think like the molecule that doesn't think; it just is. This is the nothingness of Zen, of sleep, of meditation, of stillness, of God. If God is all things, God's thought is the "thought" of molecules. Think like God just made you. Or, just as usefully: think as if the earth and the solar system, and all the elements and all the magnetic and centripetal and daily laws of energy forces made you. Now, in addition to being made, you can *think* – you who can understand these words – you can think for the Universe; possibly for the first time since God thought about it. Or, just as amazing, maybe there are others who may be stunned with the same realization.

Think like a molecule that just <u>is</u> – possibly forever.

Thinking In Molecule, Again

What is it, to think? First, it is "to be aware." Or, to begin to act – with intention, or not. Because thinking, first, at its root, is just formulation of action. We are all about conceiving, planning, executing, then conducting some analysis of knowing what's next, i.e. conceiving the next action. Dogs and fish and cockroaches can do it.

To be able, in the mind, to create action, to cause a physical change in the world – sweep a porch, paint a house, build a nest (as birds do, probably without self-consciousness, other than thoughts of action). In that way, animals think – calling out, going forward with an outcome in mind – reacting to sound, smells, words.

Voltaire said, "I think, therefore I am."

Me: "I act, therefore I 'think'."

Except, an avalanche "acts," right? Does "acting" require the existence of "intention," in the way "causing" does not. The law provides for a judgement of "manslaughter" when "causation" was present but "intention" was not.)

Don't some act unconsciously? Yes, sleep walking, and sometimes blotto drunkenness

That's an example of lower levels of thinking. The law debates the same issue; manslaughter is not murder, it is somewhat accidental, somewhat non-intentional.

Also, "innocent by reason of insanity" is a lesser degree of consciousness or sense of responsibility . . . of thinking. It seems that consciousness can have many degrees and shades, including "unconscious" and "barely conscious" and "self-conscious" and "self-less" and "contemplative" and "emotional" and "rational" and "dreaming." Whew.

But in all of those forms of consciousness, a new dawning of awareness can be cited – using a Twinkle!

It's a form of "metacognition," a stepping outside of the mental parade for a fleeting moment to say "I am watching this parade. I take notice of this cognition, this state of mind, these ideas." Then I assign (perhaps) a word, perhaps an image – some sort of "representation" of the mental event that you have noticed.

The simple act of thinking "there!" or "huh?" is enough to call it the start of a Twinkle. It's a cognition that you have noticed. And that is a beginning, of identifying and recording these identifications.

First, the structure of a Twinkle is born in the nature of an apex, a nexus, a radiating point. This then connects us to the neuronal architecture of our brain, in which nexus points connect in infinite numbers of channels to create consciousness. The twinkle joins us in a physical analogy with that real mental physical process.

The connection to writing means our thinking develops ideas more fully through a well-developed process recognized by society as valid. And esteemed.

I am a writer. My father was a famous writer. His brother, my Uncle Joe (the priest), was also a busy writer.

I mention this because my writer's brain recognizes "Twinkling" as an active part of preparing to write. It's about visualizing, defining and organizing ideas and thoughts, and creating an outline. Twinkling is a tool in this, and so of course are the words themselves (each one a Twinkle).

A number of other thinking and writing tools are very close to this topic. One is a writer's twinkling tool called Mental Mapping. This involves drawing circles with text in them, organized in a network of connections; e.g. "fishing" has branches out to sub circles that say, "lakes," "rivers," "ocean." A complete essay can be organized with these arrays of linked ideas. It's a straight shot from Twinkling; it's virtually the same process.

Another writer's tool is the "free write" in which the writer devotes exactly five or ten minutes to writing about "anything" related to the topic – essentially forcing words out on the paper to overcome mental blocks, and to suggest topics or connections with active input from the subconscious which almost gets dragged to the surface. When you free write, you are (hopefully) noticing a cascade of Twinkles, of concepts and headings for the outline, or for the diary.

And each Twinkle can be expanded into full blown "outlines" or expanding idea lists of its own.

Use the Force, Luke

This training and use of the subconscious, of the thinker's intuition, connects me to the "Star Wars" catch phrase "Use the Force Luke," as an advertisement for the use of intuition, of subconscious instincts, of free association, as a secret reserve of capability, to arrive at new realms of thinking, ideation and *action*.

A tool to represent conceptual, abstract, imaginary ideas. A tool to bridge the subconscious to the conscious and back.

First thought: Are you <u>aware</u> of it?

Then: Can you use it?

What happens when you are asleep? When you wake up?

As you go from not being aware, to being aware, the Twinkle is the first awareness. The light bulb goes on! Then, you're aware of the thought, without being worried whether it's a worthy concept, or an important one – we just want to be more aware of when thoughts come, and how can we capture them with words, or a name, or some representation that captures the idea in the here-and-now, and raising its chance of survival. We lasso the idea, the Twinkle, at first sighting; then we determine what it is, and record it or discard it.

This is a highly fluid, conceptual process. But the Twinkle does place a marker down, or a little flag gone up, or a dart in the passing rhino, indicating the presence of .

. . "A Twinkle: The First Notation." (And again, that is why it is a writing skill or habit.)

When the idea comes, are you aware of it? (If you are not aware, in essence it didn't come.) If you do notice it, can you use it? How clear is it, how memorable or indicative?

By the way: in case you didn't notice, a Twinkle is also a simple asterisk meaning: "See below for more information."

The gift of the thinking mind, the noticing mind: the gift of the possible. The universe offers this up to us, from whoever/whatever: the force, the action started it all, proved by its result: "We are, therefore we were realized." We were made – by the system, by the great maker: The Universe. There may be other dimensions, hidden and so-far-unknown histories. We are learning through all the "Twinkles," all the shining light that has blinked into being in the vast space, and in our own heads on this tiny planet. There is hope, possibility, in what we could and can create.

3

LIVING WITH A PORPOISE

We have been thinking about molecules, and about "molecular thinking" in which inspiration and the development of original thoughts are made more visually compelling – more vivid – using the conceptual tool of the Twinkle. This tool helps us tag new thoughts as they arise in the imagination, then define and develop these thoughts with writerly bullet points. The Twinkle further helps us organize the ideas into coherent structures, not unlike the way molecules assemble into materials and ultimately into living, thinking people.

These heightened levels of thinking, acknowledged using the sparkling Twinkle, touch on and even enhance the almost magical process of ideation and dawning awareness – the "ah ha!" moments of insight. The Twinkle methodically pinpoints the birth of concepts, but also suggests and helps us represent the rapid-fire, elusive nature of ideation (perhaps like the fall of snowflakes or the flash of sparks from a volcano).

I call this chapter "Living With a Porpoise" because I want to delve further into this ephemeral and often ambiguous world of thinking as we experience it in our daily lives. I suggest this with the pun of the title, a phrase which, like so much of our language and so much of our lives, implies multiple meanings and interpretations.

We humans live embedded and enmeshed in the animal world of porpoises and tigers, monkeys and microbes, and cannot live separately from it. In fact, to survive, humans must "eat life to live." We may be vegans and not eat meat, but even then we eat the products of living plants, whether fruits, vegetables or grains. We cannot survive on minerals and water alone.

Continuing to live – successfully – along with porpoises and all other forms of life is our overriding *purpose*.

And there you have the heart of our dilemma – the need and desire to coexist with our fellow living beings, and yet to acknowledge the truth of the matter – we are killers!

In this chapter, I want to build on the first two sections of the book and show how new tools can help us be more successful and to live more peaceful and cooperative lives. We are all in this together. Peaceful, rational coexistence is our only hope for planetary survival.

Nature can in fact be a brutal and uncompromising dynamic in which dogs eat dogs, and only the strong survive. Nature is "red in tooth and claw," as the poet Alfred Tennyson once wrote.

Yet as Charles Darwin has pointed out, evolution has worked because the creatures (and ideas) that survive are the ones that "fit" the best into their environments. This is what I think is meant by "survival of the fittest," not simply the survival of the strongest. (Note that the descendants of Tyrannosaurus Rex are now birds.)

How can we most naturally fit into our world in the eons to come? That is where our awareness of global warming becomes such a clear priority. We are shaping a warming environment in which mankind and countless other creatures on land and sea may soon no longer "fit." Just as atoms naturally fit or bond together based on their intrinsic natures, so must we as thinking animals, with the profound ability to understand our natural strengths and weaknesses, decide how we can evolve to reside most comfortably in our world, with minimum harm to that world and to ourselves.

Cycling back to the chapter's title: the dual meanings touch on two ideas that are equally important – our need to live in harmony with all the world's creatures, and the requirement that we understand our purpose, which is mutual survival.

If we use our tool of the Twinkle, and tag those two ideas, we discover two universes of consequence – first, cooperation and coexistence, and second survival and prosperity for all – or for most!

As in all things, we find ambiguity, contradiction and uncertainty. How do we honor coexistence when we must "eat life to live"? Do we commit to coexist with cows, pigs and chickens that shortly we will kill in order to eat and survive?

Just as challenging: how do we resolve the conflicting claims of nations for territory, or religious extremists for intellectual or spiritual domination?

It's interesting to me that Christianity seems to have addressed this conundrum, which probably exists in the subconscious mind of anyone who has ever had to cut the throat of a goat or dunk a lobster into a pot of boiling water. Killing life so that we may live is manifestly our "original sin." When, according to the story of Christianity, the Lord offered his only begotten Son as a *sacrifice* for our redemption from sin, the story resolved our guilt through an offering of the body and blood of that Son for our consumption, now in the form of bread or wafer. Our human creation of that religious story seems designed to put us at ease at the dinner table. God, we seem to have arranged him to say, allows that "It's OK for things to be this way. You can even eat my Son!"

But unlike the early-20th-century fascists, and unlike the Islamic extremists of today who clearly feel that murderous might makes right (or that "sin" must be punished), the civilized among us strive for a better balance between might and mentality. We can perhaps save our souls and maintain a good conscience by being as respectful as we can for human (and all other) life and human rights.

If only we can, in fact, be respectful!

Each person decides for him or her self whether to adopt vegetarianism as their culinary philosophy. Personally, I do what most do, which is to accept that nature has "endorsed" meat eating since creation began, when microbes began consuming other microbes. It really was the original sin. In my mind, Eve "eating the fruit of knowledge in the Garden" stands for humanity's dawning awareness of our consumptive practices. Humans had reached a point in the evolution of our consciousness that we were then aware of what we were doing (in the way that a tiger probably does *not* feel any shame or guilt for killing a zebra – and if it does, how could we ever find out?

Uncertainty and Ambiguity

Anyway, as we think with the molecules of our minds, we notice the way that in general, molecules settle themselves into arrangements that become powerful micro-actors in our world – DNA for example, or water, or our man-made metal alloys. By analyzing and reflecting on the way molecules behave, how these elements flow together, it is hopefully becoming clearer that the "analogy" of molecules and atoms in association can help us analyze, deconstruct and reconstruct our thoughts – for success. It boils down to paying attention to the actors in cause and effect.

Here, I do want to digress a bit, and say more about uncertainty and ambiguity.

There is so much we don't know about the universe, and don't know about tomorrow. We don't know how to predict what will happen. I've often been stunned at how many ways a shirt will land when I throw it onto a chair, or just how many ways a basketball will bounce when thrown at a basket.

So frankly, I am awed to think about the "molecular" nature of the amazingly complex systems that we use every day – our internet providers, our digital marketplaces, the products sold there, the numbers of consumers living in so many places. The systems and rules we follow . . . well, they aren't natural – they are human-made. It's exciting, the array of products that people can buy from Amazon or Walmart every day, across the world market. Our systems track all these exchanges of money, remember who we are, make and store and ship and save data on products moving around our world. This process supports our lives, along with our suppliers of water and removers of waste; our doctors who watch our health, plus all the systems that teach us to do these things, and learn to advance our children, and so on. Whew. We created all that with our thinking and our representational languages.

As I see it, all these human-scale activities are very much a grand extension of the world of very small particles. As Bucky Fuller said, our structured physical world is built right on another physical world of intricate tensegrities.

But, as we have also noted, even though our human systems work well, they don't work perfectly. And, the scientists can't even tell us what the world at the subatomic scale actually looks like. On one hand, it seems to be an assembly of pieces of matter. But then, bits of matter such as electrons in a water molecule, and photons and quarks, behave like fuzzy waves and fields.

These mysteries challenge scientists and other "visionaries" to create a visual and mathematical understanding of what it is actually like, so we can mentally bridge contradictory scenarios, or, as we have been doing, try to hold two mutually-exclusive ideas in our heads at the same time (which F. Scott Fitzgerald dubbed a sign of real intelligence).

It's true that sometimes we just need to accept the apparent contradictions, just as we accept the gulf between physical particles and fuzzy "wave systems" like electrons and photons.

Obviously, the nature of matter is not the only uncertainty. The future is also vague. The actual outcome of every contemplated action is to some extent uncertain. But we love it. We revel in uncertainty, right into playtime with dice, roulette wheels and lotteries.

Our vital process of communication through language is also imprecise. I may speak perfect French, but will you understand? You may tell me what happened today, but perhaps you don't remember it correctly.

Uncertainty seems to inhabit our every word; but we have dictionaries, carefully written laws, plus practical science based on careful observation and testing. Our religion also helps us deal with uncertainty, thanks to reassuring prophets and "messages" from higher beings. In our world of porpoises and buzzing flies, eagles, and human friends and enemies, we do try to live purposefully – even "porpoisefully." Like all living beings, we are striving to survive and prosper.

Crucially, for me, the Twinkle enables us to tag these vague concepts for further study. The primary way that the Twinkle is useful is in the context of understanding complex systems fraught with uncertainty. Like a good pair of binoculars, a Twinkle will spot good intuitions and ideas, and help them be understood.

The simple process of "creating-an-opening-for-a-name" gives us a chance to think artfully; what will we call this new thing?

However, here, philosopher Alan Watts rolls his Buddhist sensibilities and says that naming "objectifies" and separates us from our job of really living. I say that at that point of naming we begin to delve into new dimensions of discourse, and "see the bigger picture" thanks to vivid new descriptions and visualizations. With these tools (developed on the African savannah, right?), we travel to the far corners of the universe – as we already discussed.

My *purpose* is to use the tools of molecular thinking (perspective, appreciation of systems, appreciation of natural as well as man-made forces), along with the "meta-cognitive" tool of the thoughtfully imagined Twinkle. It can help us build a better pathway to insights and positive outcomes for life on the planet, all born out of the infinitely unpredictable and infinitely vast realm of possibilities. The basketball can even bounce *up and out* of the basket on occasion, in its dance with the hoop.

To Think Is Our Best Nature

We humans are natural creatures who live thoughtfully in the wilds of this planet, alongside many other similarly energetic living things. In just the same way as all of ife, we are born of nature and live by nature's rules first of all. But, in a sometimes confusing duality, we weave together highly developed language and logic; medicine and food production services, along with tribal warfare, murder, hatred and serious ignorance. Contradictions abound.

Even as we respond to "animalistic" urges such as rage, jealousy and instinctive tenderness towards babies, we are able to separate from our "nature" in a very important way! We can observe it, describe it and even "own" it to a degree unlike any other creature. Our thoughts and our scientific methods lead to inventions like legal contracts, money, clean bathrooms and the Hubble Telescope. We can even predict the future a bit – better than porpoises, but not perfectly.

Looking at our dual nature – thoughtful, but frequently knee-jerk reactive – might make us wonder: are we truly farther along than the porpoise? Neither we nor the porpoise see the big picture very clearly. We can't fully explain where we are, or how we got here. We can't agree among ourselves about "God" (not that the porpoise ever thinks of God that we know of), or even why we care about such things, and we certainly can't understand the worldview of the porpoise. We have made only halting steps at really communicating with the animals, but I'm sure we will get better!

Our reasoning brain can learn one thing at a time, build upon that knowledge, and travel far: perhaps one day to the point where we will know about other life in the universe, about mental powers in the universe possibly higher than our own (but also, it's true, possibly more aggressive and dangerous). Advancing in our mindful awareness and capability has got to be the purpose of our porpoise-like existence.

And it seems that we will always come to a point of starting again – as when Einstein pointed out that everything was relative, after which our physical sciences were reborn. Or when, after the ice age, humans greatly expanded their presence on the earth. There will always be new and game-changing influences. Maybe that's how we make our way to God, approaching him asymptotically, closer and closer, in steps but never quite getting there -- just as we will never know the exact value of *pi* (the ratio of every circle's circumference to the length of its own diameter). The answer can be known (3.14159 . . .), but not exactly, because the number is infinitely long!

I love Carl Sagan's idea in his novel, "Contact": that a builder of the Universe hid a secret message inside the far distant numerals of the never-ending number *pi*. In the story, Sagan's astronaut heroine learns that a (fanciful) series of zeroes and ones within the infinitely long number pi could be laid out in parallel lines to form an image of a circle.

But I get ahead of myself. And I've gotten to where we're going: It will always be useful to remember that we're living with a porpoise, balanced between sea and sky, head and heart, as we articulate and live out our dreams.

Asking *Why?* And *So What?*

So what? Ultimately, that's always the question. The child might ask "why?" The adult human says, "What do we do with this information now?"

The awareness that systems are made of parts, and the knowledge that some of the parts may be unclear or poorly understood, is one place to start seeing everything, from babbling babies to that sad wondering at graveside where we ask, "Is that all there is?"

"So what?" helps clarify the picture of us in our nicely balanced yet uncertain home. There's always a new chance to understand the bigger picture.

I hope that being open to possible new insights and new inspirations could even be a road to peace among beings of the earth, oh open-minded reader. Let us imagine, according to John Lennon's song, and build upon the hope.

Living With Everybody

Living with a porpoise; living with all of us creatures, molecules of nature, it might be useful to consider our condition and our place in the world of animals and perhaps to reimagine our relationship with them.

I have lived with Petey the dog, and many cats and other dogs, plus hamsters and fish. Horse racers know their thoroughbreds; cowboys know their cows. Knowing animals means to some degree thinking like them and imagining their minds, their desires, trying to adjust their behavior or direction, or seeking to change our direction in response to their expressed needs: ("Ok Petey, we can walk down *that* road today, if you wish.")

We don't really have a workable language with animals, which is a place where Twinkles might come in handy. When we have intuitions about their thoughts and feelings, their enthusiastic barking and insistent meows, we can at least take note. Usually, we infer meaning from the animal's posture and body language, some vocalization (such as barking), thanks to a surprisingly effective process on our part of interpreting what their clues mean. To a great extent, we can understand where the animals are coming from, even if they don't have a symbolic language to work with, and can't confirm our guesses directly.

What's obvious is that animals clearly have thinking skills that help them envision where their food is, where their homes are, and sometimes how to get into the trash can! Presumably they always know what they need in order to be happier and more comfortable.

Petey the dog always knows when he wants to lie down and stretch out in some cool grass, bring a toy to show off (for every visitor), and when he simply wants to sit and observe. He's also a very careful listener to voices and far-away barks. It's clear that he has a picture in his head of his world, and is working out his participation in it, without the benefit of actual words. It's also clear that smarts about smells play a larger role in his world view than it does in mine.

So we, and our animals, share intuition and instinct in common, a sense of place and time of day, feeling for our own needs and interests. There's a lot of common understanding, prior to any words being spoken.

Experiments have been conducted with animals to explore possible languages that could help us sync up with them more closely. A few efforts have been partially successful – and some apes have learned vocabularies of 100 words or more. Horse whisperers are famous for their equine communication skills.

The implication for me is that we are all part of this living planet. We are all born from it, oriented to the daily 24 hour rotation of the globe (creating light and dark), and programmed to its seasonal rhythms.

The partnerships that humans have helped engineer with animals are echoed in the thoughtful musings of ecology writer Michael Allaby in his book, "A Guide to Gaia:

A Survey of the New Science of our Living Earth": "If I were asked to identify a single principle that seems to guide the development of life on Earth," Allaby wrote, "I would have to call it collaboration, the establishment of mutually supportive communities." (Page 109)

Allaby thinks of these partnerships as extending from the smallest single-celled organisms joining forces to become ocean sponges, bees, and our flowers and crops, all the way up to symbiotic human communities. I link this idea to the way our human lives, partnered with pets and farm animals, potentially could be a more *active* partnership. Of course, it's a talent that we might want to take up with aliens when we meet them (and with whom we might have just as challenging a time establishing meaningful dialog).

Allaby's big idea is to see the entire Earth as a living entity. The partnership of "minds," that includes dogs, porpoises and all the other animals can perhaps begin with Twinkles standing in as allegory and allusion to the experiences of these sentient partners—helping us take notes as to the attitudes and worldview of them all.

Detailed Uses of a Twinkle

What more should we do with a Twinkle? Take heart with it. Your Twinkle of awareness is proof you're alive, producing new ideas, homing in on clarity, or at least a *hope* of clarity. "A twinkle in his eye" is a delight, a coming surprise, the beginning of new knowledge, or at least a hint of it.

Grow with it. Build with it. Develop the ideas. Map them. Define them. For all we know, the visionary consciousness we host in our heads may be the most remarkable feature of the universe (after creation itself). Whatever force or mentality or unfathomable process produced the vast reaches of everything – suns and planets! – has now, in you and me, after thirteen-plus billion years, made it possible for us to expand upon that originating work, to build upon this enormous base of existence with new ideas, new possibilities, designs and constructions and systems. And, in fact, we have been doing that.

The Twinkle is a symbol of thought that in some cases may be original. However, these days, thoughts tend to come from minds that are trained and conditioned by parents and television, by our learned language and the forces of culture, education, tradition, and habit. This is a shame, because our upward and outward and even inward-exploring and experimenting minds, with their vast number of interconnected brain cells, can think more thoughts than there are stars in the universe (we must believe). These brains represent vast new possibilities, and new hope in the universe – possibilities that could include the end of hunger, the end of war, the beginning of real and effective worldwide cooperation.

Each mind is a computer, a calculating and sorting machine, developed through evolutionary time to solve the problems of survival (breathing and eating), reproduction (finding a mate, nurturing offspring) and progress (building homes, learning to find or grow food, learning to cooperate in human culture).

At the same time, the training that the mind receives teaches us to think along familiar pathways, to move along existing roadways, either from genetic programming – like face recognition – or from cultural and parental training. Those pathways, pre-programmed with survival strategies, can actually limit our thinking – often to our detriment.

The question of free will arises. Can there actually be original thought? Can thought be free of conditioning? Of course not. Our ideas always come in the form of words that we have used many times before, represented by images that are no less familiar. We may not frequently think of things that never were seen before. But "Star Wars" and its characters and their names were all new – not preordained. So free will and originality can exist, but they come with sliding scales.

Today, we can at least imagine world peace, the end of war, the end to hunger, universal abundance and good health for all. We are tumbling and wriggling our way down those roads in world-wide quests for the cures, experiments with democracy, and the internet. Tools we can use are blooming in our hands almost faster than we can learn to use them. There is a leading edge of innovation that takes our breath away and stands for the hopeful future of humanity.

Twinkle: The Dark Side

The force behind this growth, however, is not just our conscious minds. We have cerebral mind heroes like Sherlock Holmes and Albert Einstein, but we also have beasts in our subconscious. Our heroes may actually spring from the energy and courage of our inner beasts, but so do warlike, destructive instincts that cause us to covet and to kill.

How do we continue to ride these fearsome natural steeds that live in the root power of our minds? How do we tame or more smoothly harness the wild positive energy without losing the propulsive edge it provides?

Our use of questionable energy resources such as oil, coal and nuclear power can mirror the challenges we face from our subconscious minds. While gasoline magnificently powers our cars and planes, carbon's greenhouse gases and oil spills in the oceans exact serious costs. Nuclear energy can be "clean," but it can also lead to radioactive meltdowns.

Likewise, our deep wells of mental energy that produce electron microscopes and iPhones, also produce school shooters, megalomaniacs and murderous religious fanatics.

The Twinkle Resource

Effective defenses against mental aberration have been in the works for many centuries, with legal structures regulating our societies and other security measures being the prime results. In my mind, the mental "Twinkle" is our number-one energy source for the future. It's from this power center – our human imagination – that solutions to our challenges will come. World peace and an end to hunger will not come from anywhere else (though our responses to a worldwide pandemic shows the dramatic results that can arise from an external stimulus). That's why education is such a fundamental issue. The power to think, to absorb past knowledge and synthesize it into new forms – the ability to be aware of what we are thinking so thoughts can be recorded and shared – those skills are the first step in harnessing the mental *resource* that we represent in the universe. Unfortunately, education is one of the most tortured industries on the planet. Experts flounder among themselves trying to define the methods and tools that work best.

Ultimately, education is most effective when a mind is inspired to represent itself to the world. Some level of self-awareness is born in a thinker to command and direct the internal dialogue. Unfortunately, the image of Adolf Hitler comes to mind – in his jail cell, writing his manifesto "Mein Kampf." That evil and angry soul nonetheless grasped an essential idea – that ideas must gather their energy into written words, recorded for the world to see. Most presidential candidates today start their campaign treks with a book.

Writing is next to the most fundamental moment in bringing forward ideas, virtually weightless, out of the brain-flesh, into the world. The mental-word skill is first in line to mine the Twinkle, first among all the learning trades.

But, our voice could also claim that privilege – and it does come first in the natural education of a new human (and birds and dogs as well). New life learns to speak the language of its kind.

Nor should that natural "twinkling" be overlooked in the education industry. It is so fundamental we take it for granted. But universal preschool should consider it a fundamental challenge to elevate a child's speaking skill as a key first step toward writing. Finger painting, that wonderfully messy and tactile kindergarten activity, is really a profound deployment of a writing instinct – making symbols with fingers. Maybe it deserves a new place in the education pantheon. And maybe so does voice expression, "voice painting," which could be more concrete and useful.

So, mining Twinkles through the art of writing and finger painting and vocal training, possibly voice recording and playback: what exciting activities for our preschools!

As we said, a Twinkle can stand in for the solution to any problem – like X in an algebraic equation, where X is the solution or the sought idea. Of course, X can have infinite numbers of dimensions or values that either approximate or define the solution.

Looking at a Mind Map, we see a second-step in the Twinkle process: The Twinkle at the center "imagines" (is a placeholder for) a solution. However, the possible dimensions include scenarios that would be mutually exclusive – part of the discussion, or a "straw man" – another form of a Twinkle, like a voodoo doll –but otherwise, simply ideas on the way to a solution.

In the book "This Explains Everything," edited by John Brockman (2013, Harper Perennial), I read about Claude Shannon who created a simple thesis: "Information is the resolution of uncertainty."

The Twinkle theoretically and momentarily resolves the uncertainty in the solution to any problem you might be working on, except that it is merely a placeholder.

Shannon is associated with (and effectively used) the binary number system that enabled the on-off "digital" revolution, in which information can be converted in a computer to unambiguous sets of ones and zeros A sound or a musical note can be sampled precisely in the recording studio, then translated into digital code and sent anywhere – on a CD for example – then converted back from the certain numbers into the analog sound. The accuracy of the translations, thanks to the precise and unchanging digital code, means that the recorded note plays back faithful to the original pitch and timbre. Accuracy is improved and extraneous noise is reduced.

Now, the search is on for the "quantum computer," which takes a turn toward the "messy," by seeking to run calculations – to resolve uncertainty – by <u>using</u> uncertainty in the form of quantum bits that can be on and off at the same time. This enables more potential solutions to be explored simultaneously.

To me, this is not unlike imagining a solution to a hypothetical problem of "Fred," who may be arrested if he doesn't get his life and drinking (or other bad habits) under control. Several conflicting or mutually exclusive ideas could exist in the solution window at the same time. There is uncertainty as to which might work best, but at least the potential ideas have a place to be thoughtfully examined, without being dismissed quickly.

That is one reason that the Twinkle was born in the Disney fantasy design factory, the Animation department. There, filling the air with Twinkles above Cinderella – who faced the emotional problem of how to get to the ball after her stepsisters had destroyed the gown that the helpful animals had made for her – could symbolize the arrival of a magical, hopeful solution – the arrival of a fairy godmother who created a ball gown, magical glass slippers and a coach from a pumpkin. It's charming and ridiculous, but to me the Twinkle does represent a geometric representation of an idea, a dimension-bridging vision of hope that can be defined with growing accuracy using the bullet-point spars to flesh out the idea with words and images in our real world.

It is good to place solutions in the air for hopeful study! Such placeholders should be posed for one-day solutions to ending war, ending hunger, solving the Fred problem. It's worthwhile to have a "workable space" where the hypothetical solution can be born.

The Twinkle Academy

Watching the Motion Picture Academy Awards one year (when "Gravity" and "12 Years a Slave" were winners), I was reminded what a magical, sparkling sort of enterprise it is to make a movie. A lot of very smart people work hard at separate, artistic skills, all with the goal of capturing on film discrete moments of made-up "reality." Then the best of the moments are assembled by an editor and the director in a flowing narrative using convincing visual and audio clues to enhance its veracity, its credibility.

Characters appear – players in the story. They speak and move, wearing costumes that help reinforce their roles. Countless details like sets and cars and props are arrayed in just the right view before the cameras that the image of this reality is made convincing, like a magic trick or illusion. It reminds me of the cartoon moment when Bugs Bunny paints a black arc on a canyon wall, and seconds later a train barrels out of it. It's as simple as an actor putting on a temporary disguise.

These movie-making skills continue and expand the power of the ancient storyteller who can recreate a moment in the tribal hunt when the beast was surrounded by the hunters and brought down with ropes and spears. That action is created again around the campfire through words and gestures. The tribe participates in the hunt again, perhaps experiencing the loss of one of their own in the retelling.

Today the tools are far superior – digital color and surround-sound in the theater. But the concept is the same; a few carefully arranged clues such as gesture and sound can create a moment in the mind of an observer. If these clues are carefully chosen, they can transport a mind into another place with much less effort than any physical travel. Much of our earth's population has now travelled far beyond their homes via pictures, television, Skype and interplanetary unmanned missions that delivered digital streams back to earth. As a result, we almost feel that our species has actually stood on the surfaces of Mars and the Moon, and floated among the rings of Saturn.

Thus, does our human consciousness expand into the universe, over the surface of distant planets, to the edge of the solar system and beyond.

This ability to understand hypothetical places and events – from history, or from possible futures (global warming, death of the sun) is a profound skill for our human intelligence – skill that we have little evidence is shared by other living creatures on our planet. (Though it's true that my dog can anticipate a treat when we return from a walk. On that scale, ingrained with repetition, Petey can envision something that hasn't happened yet.)

To me it's interesting that such feats of "transportation" to other realities and ideas and stories can be accomplished with very few clues – just words and pictures. With radio it's just sound – "Theater of the Mind." The action takes place in the imagination of the listener. The written word of a novel read aloud is truly a minimal stimulus.

Science fiction stories such as "A Is For Andromeda" and Carl Sagan's "Contact" imagine messages coming to earth from alien civilizations – messages that we are able to decode. Using the instructions, we are introduced to another civilization, and are trained to build a machine that can transport us far away. From "less" (an electro-magnetic signal) we get "more." From symbols and instructions we get intention, life, action, belief and birth.

I keep returning to the awesome fact that DNA is a series of clues or instructions in the form of amino acids which can be turned into organic molecules that will react at just the right time to signals coming in from the environment (i.e. sugar molecules and other food bits are all processed with waiting molecules). It's the most fantastic complex game of bowling balls reliably knocking down pins in just the right way. Or the pins being arrayed in just the right setup so as to deflect the bowling ball into just the right pocket.

The Greatest Power

What is the greatest power over the earth that controls our wind and weather and drives all the forces of life? It's the sun. After that, what is the most influential force here on earth? Arguably, except for the momentum of the rotating earth itself and its air and ocean currents, the greatest power it is the human mind.

We know that mankind's imagination and powerful hands are reshaping the planet. As a result, we are now beginning to burst forth into the Cosmos as surely as if a new sun had been born here in orbit around our sun.

That to me is the image of a Twinkle. In the same way that we see stars twinkling throughout our sky, the earth is now twinkling in our corner of the universe, sending forth electric waves and physical ships to touch the physical space and reach out to any other minds capable of noticing.

Here on the earth, our sphere is ablaze with twinkling minds, imagining the far reaches of space and the depths of our bodies, our materials, our oceans, animals and plants.

Each human mind – and those of animals too, even plants at some level – are reflecting the energy of the sun back into the void. Mankind is focusing those twinkling thoughts into physical objects, new molecules, and ideas in written words, paintings, speech, poems and film.

The second greatest force on earth – the human mind – should be seen as the force it is – coming alive in ways both good and evil.

Just as we have harnessed the atom, the petro-chemicals, the electromechanical waves – and continue to perfect those applications – the Twinkles in the imagination should be captured for goodness! "Use the force, Luke."

The Twinkle Academy recognizes that we humans can, piece by piece, construct positive realities for our living pleasure.

There is a scene in the 1999film "American Beauty," by director Sam Mendes, that is reminiscent of the lost-boy passages in the book "Catcher in the Rye." A sad misfit hero is at a shopping mall. The wind is blowing in a forlorn outside corner of the building. An empty plastic grocery bag is seen floating in a vortex of wind. The haunting feeling intrudes that all the universe includes such random forces and random movement as that loose bag swirling.

I recall hiking by myself into a canyon in Southern California that contains the east fork of the San Gabriel River. As I walked by the rushing stream, I wondered where I would establish a camp for the night. It happened about 5 p.m. that two hikers passed me on their way out of the canyon. I asked them if they knew where there might be a campground or other appropriate place to make camp. One of them said, pointing at the ground, "Hmmm; you could stay . . . there! Or there!" In other words, I was free to make my camp, wherever I thought best."

It reinforced the notion that "in the wild," a campground, a place to stay, can come at random, but circumstances of the moment, accidents, chance will probably decide things. That's how the earliest roads were built, the earliest towns established. When Adam and Eve "woke up" to consciousness, they realized they were naked in the Garden. They moved from their "animal" consciousness to their human awareness – sharper and more attuned. Our intelligence now enables us to make much better decisions, select better campgrounds, but it starts with a Twinkle of awareness.

We can all take imaginary voyages down into the molecular world, watching as furniture in the room rises up larger around us while we shrink down to the floor to run among the dust bunnies and lost pennies. Then we should shrink further, past grains of sand, past layers of grease and moisture. Small openings might appear in the floor into which we could descend like spelunkers. Small is a real place. Then we might feel the electrical charges that quiver in the floor or rug. We feel the energy in the air.

The strength of the mind is the power to envision the reality of ideas. Euclid and Descartes could see their geometries which describe our physical world, first in their minds' eyes, to be brought forth into our real worlds as drawings, explanations, structures, which in fact remain as ideas. No scaffolds were built. The lattices and trellises remain in the mind like gossamer jungle gyms on which we can walk and climb through imaginary space. So much more comes forth from that drawing room, that cave of the imagination -- Frankensteins and Draculas, highways and houses, molecules and molehills and Montana's.

Then, the issue of strength itself: can the mind hold those fleeting, flickering images long enough for them to jell into some brain-matter moment, and survive to be born onto paper as a drawing or sentence or book . . . to last, to remain, to be held and shared and considered by the group? That strength to make it real, that "vision thing" of President George Bush Sr. That map, that geography which J.R.R. Tolkien recommended should accompany any fantasy tale. Can we make it real? How about Peace? Can we make that real?

And Newton, inventing the calculus – he thought about it all the time, and finally, there it was, here it is, in the world, realized in the mind and in the computer programs as calculations, number lines. Now we even have the 3-D printer that delivers electronic concepts physically into our hands.

In Summary

So finally, what is the value, the utility, of this metaphor of the "molecule of thought," the Twinkle?

1. It serves as a reminder that we are part of the universe of physics, chemistry and the Big Bang. We are one with the totality of the Universe. We are an expression of the universe, approximately 14 billion years in the making.

2. Thinking about the forces that act on molecules, and the forces that can be delivered by molecules (such as breaking or changing the shape of other molecules) reminds us that we are part of a large system in which we act on other parts, and we, in turn, are acted upon.

3. It helps us think in terms of the energy that is all around us, that makes things work. Every molecule is defined by its energy. Energy bonds hold it together and bind the molecule into other systems. Water is a system of H_2O molecules working together fluidly according to their natures. Likewise, our natural supply of living energy is what propels us to get out of bed each morning and move forward into the day, to breathe and eat to maintain and renew our energy stores, and learn more about our environments and how best to prosper.

4. Working the metaphor of the Twinkle can lead us to new insights for action and courage. It can help us appreciate the complexity and beauty (or difficulty)

of our relationships. It may offer new perspectives on our talents and new areas in which we might decide to apply our talents.

5. The world of the molecule is ruled by logic, but also by chance. Again we say, "What goes around, comes around." This can help us be more aware that opportunity or danger can come to us at any time. Possibility is all. This, in turn, should place our attention fully in the moment, which is when things happen in our lives.

6. When we think like a molecule, we enter our universe at a new level of understanding. We are closer to the "ground floor" of knowing. The mental exercise, coupled with the embrace of uncertainty, readies us to enter our living world hopefully, with new insight, and with the ability to see ourselves more fully in our context, and in synergy with Life – again, with the hope that we can live more peacefully and fruitfully.

Can we use this metaphor, of "the Twinkle of possibility and awareness," to:

A. Imagine peace, and increasing compassion, all around the world?

B. Tag, name and describe our successes and hopeful intentions?

C. Create these hopeful ideas and visions at a more physical level?

About the Author

Chuck Champlin has been a writer and journalist; a corporate communications executive for the Walt Disney Company; a bicycle inventor; rock drummer, singer and songwriter; and a leader in California of Toastmasters clubs (public speaking) and Optimist Clubs ("Bringing out the best in kids"). He is married, and has four grown children. Chuck believes that every human being has creative contributions to make toward peace in the world. He offers the Optimist Creed (www.opmtimist.org) for the benefit of all:

Promise Yourself . . .

To be so strong that nothing can disturb your mind.

To talk health, happiness and prosperity to everyone you meet.

To make all your friends feel that there is something in them.

To look at the sunny side of everything and make your optimism come true.

To think only of the best, to work only for the best, and to expect only the best.

To be just as enthusiastic about the success of others as you are about your own.

To forget the mistakes of the past and press on to the greater achievements of the future.

To wear a cheerful countenance at all times, and give every living creature you meet a smile;

To give so much time to the improvement of yourself that you have no time to criticize others;

To be too large for worry, too noble for anger, too strong for fear, and too happy to permit the presence of trouble.

For more information about the author, you can visit his website www.champlinmedia.com or email him directly at chuck@champlinmedia.com.

BIBLIOGRAPHY

Allaby, Michael. 1989. A Guide to Gaia: A Survey of the New Science of Our Living Earth. New York: E.P. Dutton.

Brockman, John, editor. 2013. This Explains Everything. New York: Harper Perennial. (Quoting Claude Shannon).

Fuller, R. Buckminster. 1981. Critical Path. New York: St. Martin's Press.

Fuller, R. Buckminster and Robert Marks. 1973. The Dymaxion World of Buckminster Fuller. Garden City, New York: Anchor Press/Doubleday.

Harold, Franklin M. 2003. The Way of the Cell: Molecules, Organisms, and the Order of Life. New York: Oxford University Press.

Sargent, Ted. 2006. The Dance of Molecules: How Nanotechnology Is Changing Our Lives. New York: Thunder's Mouth Press.

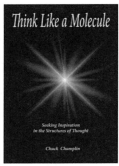

Think Like a Molecule: Seeking Inspiration in the Structures of Thought
by Chuck Champlin
AuthorsPress

book review by Tony Espinoza

One of the things you learn in high school and college is that one of the basic building blocks of life and matter overall in the universe are molecules. Molecules make up everything, from the stars themselves to everyday people. As Tom Noddy once said, "It's an electrical network, isn't it? It's molecules in space... and they're linked to each other electrically. Which is to say, one end of a soap molecule is attracted to a nearby water molecule electrically. The bubble is this network. The whole thing is inter-dependent."

In author Chuck Champlin's Think Like a Molecule: Finding Inspiration in Connection and Collaboration, the author explores the world of molecules in a unique and powerful way. Author Chuck Champlin seeks inspiration through deep and imaginative journeys from within the vast and varied realms of the cosmos themselves through the exploration of molecules. From the science of molecules and their function in the universe to the infinite possibilities that arise when exploring and thinking like a molecule, which allows the author and by proxy us readers the ability to be aware of the physical foundations that have in turn given rise to our very thoughts.

This is a read that involves a lot of self-exploration, from understanding the science of molecules and their behavior to how these building blocks could create even more possibilities within our universe and everything in between. The author writes a powerful and extensive read in a short amount of time, and yet will leave a lasting impression on the reader. This thought-provoking book does an excellent job of showcasing the contrast between the accidental nature that billions of molecules came together to make us, and yet allowed our formed minds to be capable of creating new and exciting new things to populate our universe.

This is the perfect book for those who enjoy scientific and philosophical ventures, and non-fiction reads which challenge and compel the reader to explore notions that may be outside of their own comfort systems. As a reader with an interest in possibility and the unknown, it was fascinating to see this author's journey down this path of exploration that showcases how the worlds of science and philosophy are more connected than many previously believed.

Intense, thought-provoking and educational, the author pushes boundaries and explores concepts and ideas directly tied into the nature of molecules and what they in turn have created that are far beyond the imagination of most of us readers. This is one of those rare books that pushes the reader to reach beyond themselves and what they already know, and delve into the unknown without any guarantee of a definitive answer to some of life's most challenging questions. A lot of critical and key information and philosophical questions posed within a short amount of time, this is a book that readers will not want to miss.

US Review
of Books

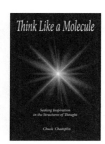

Think Like a Molecule: Seeking Inspiration in the Structures of Thought
by Chuck Champlin
AuthorsPress

book review by Michelle Jacobs

"Thinking like a molecule is an opportunity to notice the way bits and pieces of our world combine to make new arrangements, which can have important effects."

Champlin's book is a celebration of the power and possibilities of human thought and imagination. The author uses molecules as a metaphor for creating something new out of our personal experiences and connections to others. As such, the universe becomes a rich reflection of humanity's pursuit of understanding and progress. Inspired by his work at Disney Studios, Champlin has also created a conceptual tool to convey the thinking process and the imaginative spark needed to develop ideas. He calls this the Twinkle, which is not quite a light bulb but a placeholder for a newly arriving thought or idea. A Twinkle is a glimmer of thought that needs more time and focus to shine brighter. Twinkles have the possibility and power to impact individuals as well as communities or even the entire world. Champlin hopes that raising the quality of our thinking and making space for ideas and imagination will lead to peaceful co-existence, problem-solving, and purposeful, intentional living.

Using personal anecdotes and research, the author displays a verdant mind rich with references and associations that support curiosity and exploration across disciplines. Thinkers and writers from a wide range of fields of study like nanotechnology, physics, biomimicry, and animation are collected and combined to elucidate Champlin's call to think like a molecule. Clearly, he is devoted to learning as he models the very thing he celebrates, making connections in pursuit of new ideas and understanding. For example, Champlin writes, "Thinking like a molecule means noticing how physical things and people come together, how they work in combinations, and imagining new ways that those combinations can be replicated and improved. Thinking like a molecule may give us new perspectives on things we take for granted and inspire new thoughts about the assembly of our world." Ultimately, the author sees the potential in all of us for betterment as individuals and collectively.

His hopeful, urgent call to imagine possibilities for ourselves and our world is inspiring and thought-provoking. Champlin's engaging, charming voice is confident and playful, and his ability to break down his molecular view of the world is powerful and full of insight. Many writers have seen the metaphorical value of nature and write lyrically about the processes of trees, flowers, rivers, and the seasons as mirrors for human struggles, cycles, and behavior. Champlin achieves a similar feat at the molecular level. His purpose is not to explain the universe but to inspire with the universe's foundations applied to human endeavor. With cogent, compelling prose, Champlin offers up a unique perspective of what it means to think like a molecule, which "can help us build a better pathway to insights and positive outcomes for life on the planet, all born out of the infinitely unpredictable and infinitely vast realm of possibilities."

While Champlin acknowledges the stumbling blocks to igniting and following twinkles of thought, his message is hopeful and helpful. Uncertainty and ambiguity exist in human systems but should not be impossible barriers that cannot be overcome. With Champlin's treasure trove of ideas, insight, and grounded wisdom, our minds can embark on infinite possibilities of thought, for "to think is our best nature."